*for Moms and Minivan Drivers

Soccer For Moms*

game & parenting essentials
for healthy kids

by **Kerrie Paige**

plain white **press**™

WHITE PLAINS, NY

Help us make this book better!

The *For Moms*™ series of books is written by moms to help parents. We value your feedback and advice for revisions and additions to the next printing and on our website. We're also looking for your best funny or instructive Soccer Mom stories. If we use your suggestion, we'll send you a free copy of the next edition.

Go to: PlainWhitePress.com/4Moms

LCCN: 2009928436
ISBN 978-0-9815004-3-0

Plain White Press books are available at special discounts when purchased in bulk for premiums and sales promotions, as well as for fund-raising and educational use. Special editions or book excerpts can also be created to specifications. For details contact Publisher@PlainWhitePress.com

Manufactured in the United States of America

Dedication
For Coleman, Alex, and Nick,
who've made it fun to be a Soccer Mom
but a complete joy to be a mother

Acknowledgements

When a goal is scored in soccer, one person is given primary credit, but in reality it has been achieved through the combined work of a team. Writing a book is no different. Thanks to Julie Trelstad, publisher at Plain White Press, for creating the concept of *Soccer for Moms* and the *For Moms*™ series, but especially for being so much fun to work with. Designer Katie Schlientz created a beautiful layout that really made the text come alive. Editors Roberta Hendry and Graham Trelstad worked overtime to attend to the details. Marketing manager/Soccer Mom Angel Tinnirello provided valuable insights and is waiting to take the ball as soon as it is printed. My Soccer Mom friends have shared their ideas and taught me so much along the way. Soccer Moms Cheryl Hennesey, Selena Paulsen, and Donna Snyder have provided particularly helpful insights and input. Kirsten Smith helps me keep the mom juggling act going smoothly. My parents, Wayne and Suzie Conklin, were my first, and best, soccer parent role models. They went cheerfully to countless games and practices and continue to be amazing supporters for their grandkids. My brother, David Conklin, and sister, Kathy Jacobson, helped me learn to play, set me straight where needed, and have been beyond supportive in all things. While we're on the topic of supportive, I would put my husband, Jaret Hauge, up against anyone as most supportive husband ever. He's had to pick up a lot of slack over the past several months and has always done so cheerfully. And last but not least, my sincerest thanks to my boys, who never once complained about all of the hours that I spent writing this book, and who never failed to share great ideas when I asked for their input.

Table of Contents

1 Introduction

Sports aren't like they were when we grew up. There are many more pressures. Kids are over-scheduled and over-specialized. All of this leads to a whole new set of concerns for the moms who are trying to keep them happy and healthy, while maintaining their own sanity. Because you are holding this book, I'm guessing you're one of them.

If you are anything at all like me, you are already suffering from lack of time and information overload. At the same time, you've got questions and you want to get a handle on the sport that is occupying a good part of your family's life. That's why we've developed this book to be both comprehensive and quick to skim. You'll find answers to frequently asked questions and useful tips in easily identifiable sidebars throughout. You'll also find a handy glossary to quickly translate all those strange

soccer terms you'll hear tossed about.

If your family is completely new to soccer, I recommend that you start at the very beginning and work your way through. See an area that has more detail than you want for now? No problem. You can just skip ahead, knowing that the information will be there to come back to when you need it.

If you have been doing the soccer thing for a while now, you may want to start at Section 3, *Let's Play*, where we'll provide some more in-depth background to further your enjoyment of the game. Section 4 is your tournament survival guide. In Section 5, we'll give you all the dirt on the equipment your family needs, and some it doesn't need but might want nevertheless. In Section 6, we'll take a close look at how to keep your player safe, well-fed and hydrated. Section 7 tackles the important question of how to work with your child's coach to create a positive experience for everyone. In Section 8, I'll share a number of tips and tricks I and my fellow Soccer Moms have picked up over the years to keep our balance and sanity during the soccer season. Section 9 provides a sneak-peek of what life is like for an elite level soccer player. Finally, at the end of the book, you'll find a convenient reference section with a glossary and a list of resources for further reading.

It is my sincere hope that this book will make your life as a Soccer Mom more enjoyable and easier to manage.

P.S. Along the way, I've illustrated points with stories from my experience and the experiences of other moms I know. I'm guessing that you have your own stories and tips as well. We'd love to hear about them! Please share with us and other Soccer Moms by visiting PlainWhitePress.com/4Moms. *If we use your suggestion, we'll send you a free copy of the next edition!*

WHO THIS BOOK IS FOR

There has been a lot of talk about Soccer Moms over the past few years. Who does she vote for? What does she buy? But there hasn't been a book with the practical, specific, from-the-trenches information geared specifically toward helping her BE a better Soccer Mom: more knowledgeable, more prepared, more organized and, therefore, ready to have more fun! If a kid you care about plays soccer, this book is for you!

There are many fine books about how to play soccer, the rules of soccer, the greatest heroes of soccer, and how to coach soccer. There even are a number of good how-to-parent-young-athlete books. The goal of this book is to provide you with the real-world, practical, mom-tested advice you need to parent your soccer player with skill and grace—or at the very least a sense of humor! While I will, of course, cover game basics, even these topics will be slanted toward the parent's perspective.

MOMS I KNOW WHO NEED THIS BOOK

When writing this, I've tried to keep several prototype readers firmly in mind. The first prototype is based on one of my oldest and dearest friends. She grew up in an area where soccer wasn't such a big thing yet (very common when most of us who are now raising kids were growing up). As a result, she didn't play, nor did she have many friends who played. She's smart, she's supportive, and she's even athletic. She just hasn't had a lot of experience with soccer and, therefore, doesn't always understand all of the game's nuances. Her kids have shown some real talent, so she's accepted the fact that she's likely to spend something approximating the rest of her natural life in the vicinity of a soccer field. Because she's analytical by nature, she has the feeling that she'd enjoy the process a little more if she really understood what was going on. She also is a single working mother and is happy to learn all of the time-saving tips anyone cares to share.

At the other end of the spectrum is my wonderful, incomparable sister. Like me, she can't remember NOT being around a soccer field. She started playing in preschool and hasn't stopped since. As the youngest of three kids in a soccer family, she was so far ahead of the game that she preferred to play on boys' teams until she was 10 or so (and, incidentally, was usually the best player on the team). She has been a player and a fan of the game for years now. She knows all of the rules; she knows about league structures, how tournaments work, and even what it takes to win a college soccer scholarship, because she did in an era when there were few to win. But with all of this deep soccer knowledge and skills (she still can hit a killer strike from the edge of the box), the fact remains that she's not yet had the pleasure of getting to raise a soccer player, and that's a different thing entirely. She is now mom to three young daughters, the oldest of which is just starting to play soccer. My goal is to provide some useful information in these pages that even she doesn't know.

This book has been designed to cover the needs of both of these moms and every mom in between. Yes, there is a section that explains in straight-forward language such important topics as the oft-confusing offside rule and how a midfielder's role differs from a forward's. The expert mom may very well choose to skim this section or skip it altogether (but I would point out that some of the rules we played with growing up have changed).

Even though some readers already may have a great handle on the game basics, we all can use a helping hand when it comes to anything related to parenting. To make sure that I am passing along a balanced perspective, I have interviewed many other long-time Soccer Moms who have graciously shared their experiences with me. My goal is to provide you with readily accessible, immediately useful information that is easy to put into practice in your real life with all of its hiccups and frantic moments. Simply put, I aim to tell it to you straight. You won't find general theoretical how-it-should-be-done advice from my extensive book research unless the advice also has proven itself useful to either my family or the families of my Soccer Mom advisors. For that reason, I hope that *Soccer for Moms* will have something for everyone, much of which has never been compiled and presented in this way ever before.

WHY MOMS?

Now to address the question that my all-male children keep asking me: What's so special about moms? Why not write a book for all parents of all genders? First, I would argue that moms *are* special. I know and respect a great many Soccer Dads and know that they care about supporting their kids in the best way possible too. But I also believe moms are different. We have unique concerns and interests, and simply look at the world at a different angle than the dads. Some of the things we worry about would make the Soccer Dads shake their collective heads. But worry about them we do, and so they deserve to be addressed in a book for Soccer Moms.

Second, having spent the past 15 years as a Soccer Mom, the Soccer Mom is a species I understand. I have tallied uncounted miles and minutes in soccer-related activities. I have spent many a February shivering in a heavy rainstorm wondering why I didn't steer my kids toward basketball or some other sport civilized enough to be played in the cheery warmth of a gym. I have made many last-minute trips to the grocery store for oranges because I forgot—again—that it was my turn on the dreaded snack list. Over the years, my social circle has gradually morphed until it has become disproportionately populated by other Soccer Moms. Just wait—it will happen to you too, if it hasn't already. Let's just say that I've been living the life of a Soccer Mom for a long time and can therefore speak authentically to her needs. I have also been extremely fortunate to have had the opportunity to pick the brains of scores of other Soccer Moms. Many have graciously shared all of the things they know now, but wish they knew back at the beginning. I hope, too, that there is a great deal of information for them.

GAME PLAN FOR MOMS—OUR PHILOSOPHY

When all is said and done, soccer is a game. Period. It can teach our kids many valuable lessons. It can help develop a lifelong active lifestyle, and it can help provide a healthy social outlet. But in the end, the reason we choose to send in that very first registration form is because we hope that our kids will have fun. Too many over-anxious parents forget that. I've certainly been guilty of it myself from time to time.

I once had the fortunate experience of attending a lecture by an experienced coach named Bruce Brown. I didn't know that I was going to be listening to the lecture. In fact, I half expected it would be an unnecessary time drain. (After all, I had stuff to DO!) Mr. Brown had been brought in by the board of the travel team club in our area as part of an orientation for new parents. I'd been involved with soccer for a good 30 years by that point. I imagined I'd have heard it all before.

This was a number of years ago, and I can't remember most of what Mr. Brown said, but I will always remember one simple, but very profound, statement. He explained that when he talked with some of his most successful students years later about

Enjoy the Game

What matters is that your child is free to enjoy the game. My philosophy is that your job is to support your player and to provide him or her with the general skills to be a good student of the game. Other than that, you can sit back, relax, and enjoy what you will surely look back on as some of the fondest memories of your life. It is a game. Soccer is a beautiful, fascinating game, but a game nonetheless. Release your child to it.

what had helped them most in their careers, he noticed a common theme. They told him that the important adults in their lives had been most supportive simply by letting the player, well, play. To sum up his point, Mr. Brown said, "If there is only one thing that you take away from this night, please remember this: Release your player to the game."

This advice can be hard to remember when the score is 1-1 heading toward overtime in an important match, and you wish your child would play just a little bit harder, or when you completely disagree with a substitution that the coach has just made. It is easy, too, to get wrapped up into thinking that a certain tournament win really matters. In the end, almost none of it does matter, except whether or not your child enjoyed the experience.

WHY SHOULD MY CHILD PLAY?

Before we dive into details, let's step back for a moment and consider why you should fill out that registration form in the first place. Let's face it—there are many, many activities competing for your child's attention and for a share of the family budget. Why choose soccer?

If you have any doubt as to whether soccer is worth your family's time, effort and resources, consider the many benefits. Your child's physical, mental and emotional well-being may just be the better for it.

IS SOCCER RIGHT FOR MY CHILD?

In a word—yes! Soccer is unique among sports in that it is universally suitable for just about every child. Is your child destined to be a little more petite than average? No problem. Great soccer players come in all sizes. Is your child shy, or embarrassed to be singled out? The average soccer team provides a great supportive platform for helping a shy child to flourish.

If somebody loses a ball here and there, it is almost never tragic and certainly isn't as embarrassing and in-your-face obvious as, say, dropping an infield fly in baseball. In soccer, all players are connected in an ever-changing, fluid way, making it easy to feel supported and an integral part of the whole team. With the ability to contribute in many concrete and meaningful ways in each game and practice, soccer can help establish a strong sense of self-esteem and belonging in even the most introverted wallflower.

Compared with other youth enrichment activities—unless your family decides to pursue very high-level play with its high travel costs—soccer is relatively inexpensive. The equipment list required is smaller and less expensive than many other team sports. To be fair, though, I should emphasize the words *relatively* inexpensive. It would be inaccurate to claim that soccer won't put at least a small dent in the family budget. Sports may be expensive, but they are a worthwhile investment because they keep kids out of trouble.

The sport is very simple to teach even very young children, yet it is rich enough to support a lifetime of continued learning. It also is enormously open to adaptation. Change the field sizes, simplify the rules slightly, and you can easily accommodate any age and many developmental disabilities.

It May Not Be For Everyone

While soccer is a great option for just about all children, there are a few who just don't connect with the sport, especially when very young. I have heard from several moms that soccer was so popular and so much a part of the social structure of their area that they felt a pressure to participate, even though their children weren't enjoying themselves. If you find yourself in this situation, please, by all means, do not push the issue.

THE UPSIDE OF ACTIVITY

According to a report issued by the U.S. Department of Health and Human Services in 1995, high school students who participated in any form of organized extracurricular activity were:

* 57 percent less likely to drop out of school
* 49 percent less likely to have used illegal drugs
* 37 percent less likely to have become teen parents
* 35 percent less likely to have smoked cigarettes
* 27 percent less likely to have been arrested

Health Benefits

There are many physical, mental, and emotional benefits to being part of a team. Should you ever wonder, bleary-eyed and sore-bummed from driving carpool yet again, why exactly you're doing all this, turn back to this section as a reminder. Any single one of the well-documented benefits below would make it all worthwhile—and remember this is just a very small sample. The evidence is clear and compelling.

Athletes do better in school

* Multiple studies over many years have shown that, contrary to the dumb jock stereotype, student athletes tend to have higher grade point averages than their non-athlete counterparts. *Shape* Magazine reports that "A study at Michigan State University found that teens who played sports scored 10 percent higher on standardized tests than their inactive peers. Physical activity increases blood flow to the brain, which improves memory and concentration."

* Sports can even help some kids manage learning disabilities. It is well known that regular exercise can help kids manage the symptoms of ADD. Many kids even see a degree of improvement that rivals the use of prescription medication.

Kids are healthier—physically, mentally, and emotionally

* Sports are good for overall mental health. Regular exercise helps kids manage stress, avoid depression, and keep a healthy perspective.

* According to some studies, children who participate in soccer have a tendency toward higher bone density and higher lean muscle mass than their counterparts who participate only in a standard gym class.

* The National Association of Sports and Physical Education pro-

motes **structured** daily physical activities for young children of 60 minutes or more and up to 60 minutes of unstructured play per day. Soccer is an excellent example of just such a structured activity.

✱ According to the American Academy of Podiatric Sports Medicine, children active in sports programs improve their cardiovascular and musculoskeletal systems, state of mind, and coordination.

LEADERSHIP AND TEAMBUILDING

As a team sport, soccer offers an abundance of leadership opportunities in both subtle and not-so-subtle ways. The most obvious opportunity for a child to fill a leadership role on a soccer team is to be nominated as a team captain. That honor usually goes to one or two players at a time and may not be used at all on very young teams.

Luckily there are many less visible opportunities available as well. Perhaps one child catches on to a fundamental skill a little faster than another and graciously offers to help the other. On another day, a different player may unwittingly inspire others by giving her best during a practice. Yet another child may make the choice to be gracious and a good sport in a difficult situation. The possibilities are endless.

By the very nature of the sport itself, members of a soccer team must depend on each other in order to be successful. After the age of six or so, no matter how much of a hotshot a kid on the opposing team may be, it is easy enough to stop him if you send enough of your team's players to defend against him. The only way to be consistently successful is to work together. This naturally, but effectively, teaches teamwork.

POSITIVE USE OF TIME

Whether you choose soccer or another sport, try to find an organized athletic activity of some kind. According to the American

Academy of Pediatrics the average child watches three hours of television per day. Clearly, the average child has room in his or her life for something more constructive!

Anecdotally, I can say that kids who are actively involved into their teenage years have much less of a tendency to get into trouble. It is easy to see why this might be. When he was 15, one of my sons was playing on three teams at a time, one of which held practices one and a half hour's drive away. I didn't have to worry much about what trouble he was getting into because he simply didn't have time. Even had he had enough time,

Life Lessons

Without getting overly philosophical, let me point out that there are many life lessons to be found on a soccer field.

* The better side doesn't always win, but given enough shots they'll prevail more often than not. Everyone makes mistakes.

* The best way to progress toward a goal is by making the best use of the unique skills of those around you.

* Hard work and perseverance really do pay off.

* No matter how talented a collection of individuals may be, they will never truly shine until they work together.

* You can learn more from a wise, experienced, and insightful coach or teammate than from hours of struggle on your own.

* Being accountable to both yourself and your teammates helps everyone succeed.

* Losing isn't the end of the world. In fact, most losses are forgotten roughly two seconds after the next win.

* Being a good sport feels a lot better than getting by on cheap shots. A win unearned doesn't feel much like a win in the end.

* And last but not least, a shootout is a heartbreaking way to lose a hard-fought game. (There must be a life lesson in there somewhere!)

© ISTOCKPHOTO.COM/DALTON00

he almost certainly would not have had enough energy! While this may be a somewhat extreme example, the fact remains—kids who are at soccer practice are not getting into trouble or engaging in risky behaviors.

BUILDS LONG-TERM RELATIONSHIPS WITH FRIENDS AND FAMILY

There also is the social aspect to teambuilding. Some of my longest lasting friendships were formed on the soccer field, and the same has been true for my own boys. My 17 year old, as I write this, is out with one of the teammates from his first-grade team. They no longer play on the same team, but they are still great friends. This tendency toward long-term friendships, incidentally, is a factor that you should keep in mind when choosing where your child will play. As several moms I interviewed pointed out, if you allow your child to play for a neighboring town, be prepared to drive there a lot over the next few years for social activities, as well as soccer.

Like it or not, you, too, will be spending many, many weekends in the company of other parents in the local soccer community. You might as well make the most of it and befriend your fellow parents now. You're all in this together, and you'll be able to help each other in many ways. You'll also have a lot more fun during your many hours on the sidelines. Among my closest circle of friends, I have soccer ties with nearly all of them.

My family was a soccer family long before most people in this country had even heard of the sport. I can't remember a time when warm-weather Saturdays weren't devoted to the sport. My brother, sister, and I all played from early elementary school through college and on into the adult leagues. Dad coached at times. Even Mom got in on the act, joining one of the first adult women's leagues in the early '70s. We enjoyed family outings to professional soccer games and team parties. Across the years, soccer always provided a common ground and shared interest for all of us—a benefit that continues to this day as we all gather whenever we can to cheer on the next generation.

And it's not only the kids who get to have all of the fun. Thanks to the boom in recent years in college intramural and local adult leagues, soccer can be a lifelong sport. I continued to play in adult leagues for many years until sidelined by an injury, but I hope to return sometime soon. For a number of years, I had the privilege of playing on an adult team with my mother. Just last year, she played on a team that won a regional over-60 tournament!

Fun!

I've saved this reason for last to make a point. I believe that fun should always be the bottom line to your child's participation in soccer or any other sport. They are *kids* and they are supposed to be having fun. As kids get older and the level of competition increases, this can be an extremely difficult thing to remember at times. When the time comes—and it will—that you are tempted to yell at a ref, or worse, at your child, please remember that this is supposed to be about fun.

MY LIFE AS A SOCCER MOM

I can't remember NOT being around a soccer field. First, I was a soccer sibling. Some of my first memories involve sitting on a blanket watching my five-year-old brother and his friends play in one of the nation's very first youth soccer leagues. Like any kid with a healthy dose of sibling rivalry, I insisted that I get to play too. I did and—fell in love.

I continued playing through high school and on into college. I was fortunate enough during that time to get to travel to many tournaments, and to play with many talented players, culminating in an appearance in the NAIA National Collegiate Championships with the University of Puget Sound. My three boys came along shortly thereafter, and I made the gradual transition from soccer player to Soccer Mom and soccer coach. I took a brief break from playing when my boys were small, but

Kerrie at age 7—all suited up and ready to play.

Kerrie with her two younger boys who are still active on the soccer circuit.

then rediscovered the fun in a local adult league.

I've been a proud Soccer Mom for more than 15 years now. There have been points when it began to feel like it was nearly a full-time job (which was tiring, given that I'd always had another full-time job too—in my other life, I am a mathematician and run an international consulting company). During the soccer careers of my three boys, I've parented across the full range of possibilities offered by youth soccer today; from recreational three-a-side teams of four year olds to high school to state- and regional- champion elite club teams. While I haven't been a college Soccer Mom yet, I can attest to the experience, as my siblings and I all were college players. I also spent a number of years coaching my boys when they were ages 4 through 12.

In short, if it has to do with youth soccer, chances are very good that I have been exposed to it at some point, either as a player, parent, or coach. My knowledge is also current. As of this writing, my two youngest boys, ages 13 and 17, are still deep into youth soccer. And I mean that very literally—many of these pages were written during one of the thousands of soccer practices I have attended.

2 Where Do We Start?

The media image of Soccer Moms may portray us as sitting serenely around (because we have nothing better to do) in our designer track suits while we sip **half-caf-nonfat-no-whip-mocha lattes.** Well, that's not what I'm like, nor is it what any of my many Soccer Mom friends are like. I'm betting that's not what you're like either. I bet that you picked up this book because you suspect that there is a lot of juggling, parenting, consuming, planning, cheering, and life lessons that go into being a stellar Soccer Mom, and you don't want to have to learn everything the hard way.

Being a Soccer Mom is a multi-faceted job, and there's a lot to cover—much more than I bet you would imagine if you are new to the sport. Along the way we'll anticipate and answer the

wide range of questions that are likely to come up during your career as a Soccer Mom.

* **Understanding the Game Itself:** What is the coach talking about? Why did the referee blow his whistle? What can I expect at my first game?

* **Understanding the Parenting Issues:** How do I feed a growing soccer player? What if she's not getting along with the coach? What if she wants to quit? Should we give the travel program a try? How soon?

* **Mastering the Logistics:** What kind of time and money commitment are we talking about? How do I choose between the bewildering array of equipment options, and more important, what does my child *really* need, and what can she do without?

Don't worry—we'll talk about all of that and much more in due course. But we have to start somewhere. When you sign up your kindergartner for her first soccer experience, you probably aren't worried just yet about whether or not she should try out for the State Olympic Development Program or how much an out of state tournament is likely to cost you—at least I sincerely hope you aren't! You are probably wondering what soccer is all about, how it works, and what you can expect at the very beginning. That's what this section will cover. If you are well into your career as a Soccer Mom, this book still has a lot for you, but you can feel free to skip this first section. We'll get to all of the details for more advanced soccer players later.

Your First Day as a Soccer Mom

It is not entirely clear where we should mark your first day as a Soccer Mom: Is it when you first sign up, or perhaps, the first game? I'd argue that it really all begins in earnest with the first practice session. Leading up to that first day, though, there will have been a sequence of events that went something like this:

* You'll get a call or an email from some (hopefully) kind soul who has volunteered to coach, unless of course, *you* are that kind soul who volunteered to coach. You'll probably receive some sort of a short introduction to a coaching philosophy, and details about the team's practice schedule. Don't be surprised if you are also encouraged to volunteer to serve in one of several important capacities, such as team mom.

* Your son or daughter (or I suppose possibly both for those of you with multiples!) will begin to ask daily when they get to buy their first new pair of soccer shoes and other equipment.

* After stalling the dreaded shopping trip as long as possible (or is that just me?), you load your child into the car for a visit to the nearest soccer shop or sporting goods retailer. He might beg for a tiny version of the same cleats he's seen his favorite pro star wearing, but you can resist, knowing that really isn't necessary just yet. You'll probably pick up basic cleats, shinguards, long practice socks, soccer shorts, a ball, and possibly a re-usable water bottle. (See the extensive chapter on equipment for all you ever possibly wanted to know about how to make these choices.)

* Depending upon your local league, you might have a pre-season parents meeting. These are very common for older age groups, particularly among travel teams, but not so common for young recreational leagues.

Before you know it, your first official day as a Soccer Mom will arrive. Hopefully it will be a nice sunny afternoon when you don't already have to be in 47 other places. (We can hope, can't we?) When you are getting your child ready for practice, make sure she's dressed comfortably, preferably in layers, and is wearing shinguards, long socks, and cleats. Don't forget the sunscreen if you really did get the sunny day we were all hoping for, and send along a ball if you have one handy.

WHAT HAPPENS WHEN YOU ARRIVE ON THE SCENE

It's a good idea to arrive a few minutes early to allow your child to adjust to the new surroundings. Many practice locations happen to have playgrounds. I haven't seen a six-year-old yet who didn't find this a distraction. If they get a few minutes on the playground first, it won't compete for their attention later.

The other players will start arriving gradually. Coaches who are in tune with six-year-old attention spans will provide a simple activity to keep players busy while players are arriving. After the first few sessions, it will probably be a simple passing game, but before the coach has had a chance to explain any of that, they may start with something basic like a game of tag.

Which brings me to an important point—don't expect practice sessions to resemble the sport of soccer for the first few sessions. Current guidelines from the U.S. Soccer Federation encourage coaches of really young players to promote a lot of free play both with and without the ball. The kids will have lots of fun and improve their general fitness and balance, while still getting a gentle introduction to basic ball skills. There will be lots of time for formal play with rules as they continue on.

Once all have arrived, the coach will introduce himself, talk a little bit about the year ahead, and then dive right into play. You'll probably see them play a few games designed to get them moving, laughing, and getting a feel for the ball. After a short 30-45 minutes, the practice will end, and—if the coach has done her job well—your child will beam the whole way home.

Because it is so important to keep all of the players active and involved, coaches of very young teams can make good use of parent-helpers. If you are willing to help with crowd control, be sure to let the coach know. You don't need to know anything at all about soccer to be a great help. You can chase down loose balls, keep a small group going on the current activity, or generally act as a second set of hands—or feet as the case may be.

LEARNING THE LANGUAGE OF SOCCER

Soccer is much like chess in that anyone can pick up the basic rules in a few minutes, but even life-long students of the game continue indefinitely to learn about the game's finer points.

There are infinite nuances to strategy, movement, and skill that will unfold over time and support a lifetime of learning and enjoyment. It is no accident that Pelé—one of the most talented players ever to grace the pitch—proclaimed soccer to be the beautiful game.

What's a pitch, you ask? Not to worry, I've included a glossary that you can use as a reference if you come across strange terminology. Soccer has plenty of unique expressions. I'll go ahead and use those words throughout the book, but I promise, also, to provide you with clear and simple explanations as needed. So here's our first lesson: The pitch is the field of play—arguably soccer's most important element. We'll talk all about the pitch, its sizes, and its surfaces in a later section.

WHAT IS A U10?

The first strange soccer terms that you'll come across are the abbreviations used to designate age divisions. Instead of *nine-year-old age division,* the age group will be called *Under-10* and abbreviated as *U10.* Why not just use the former? It is because the actual age of kids on a team can be mixed and a bit fuzzy. It isn't exactly fair to have a nine year old playing on a team of six year olds, but there are cases where it might make sense for a precocious five-year-old to start a bit early and play up. To account for these situations, league rules will state that players for a given age division must have been born on or before a specific date. In other words, instead of saying that players must be six years old, the rules will specify that players must be *Under 7* as of a certain date, usually at the beginning of the fall season, but sometimes December 31. The date most often used is July 31. So, if your child is six years old as of July 31, she would play in the U7 league. If her birthday happens to be August 1, this would mean that she'd be seven years old for most of her U7 season.

Why can't my daughter play with her classmates?

Soccer age group divisions don't usually correspond to the age cut-offs used by school districts. While school age cut-offs vary throughout the country (ranging from August 31 to December 1 for the most part), they almost never match the common soccer cut-off dates of July 31 or December 31. Any kids with  birthdays in the gap between the two cut-offs will end up playing with kids in another grade. This is what happened with me. My school district in Southern California used a December 1 cut-off, but the soccer cut-off was December 31. My late December birthday made me too young for the next grade up, but too old to play with the vast majority of kids in my own grade. The result was that I played with girls one school grade up for my entire youth career.

You might not like the idea of your child playing with kids in another grade, but it can have its upside. In my case, I enjoyed the chance to make friends with a group that I normally wouldn't have. And as a bonus, it really helped smooth the transition to middle school and high school because I already had many friends there.

LEAGUE STRUCTURE

When you first consider signing your child up for soccer, you might never guess just how big of a world is opening up for both of you.

Your child will have the opportunity to stay active, make friends, and have fun. And so will you, for that matter. On the other hand, you could also end up spending a ton of money, hanging out with overly intense people, and driving around so much that it isn't any fun. The trick for making your soccer years the best possible experience is to choose the right level of involvement for your family.

When you hear other moms bemoan the incredible amount of money they spend on soccer or the amount of time it takes up, you might fear that any soccer involvement will eventually lead you down the slippery slope to over-involvement. It doesn't have to be that way. There are many playing options to choose from, each of which comes with its own level of expense and time commitment.

Recreational soccer is generally fairly inexpensive, with registration fees in the $50-$75 range for an eight-week season. The time commitment is also minimal; you can expect one to two short practices per week, plus one game at a nearby field for two short eight-week seasons per year. In a recreational league, everyone is welcome, and everyone is given lots of playing time.

At the other extreme are the highly competitive club travel teams. By the time you add in registration fees, equipment costs, coaching stipends, tournament fees and travel costs, it is not uncommon for a family to spend in excess of $3,000 per player per year on travel soccer. The concept of a season doesn't mean much anymore at this level. Many travel team players are playing year-round or very close to it. Because tournaments and games are played across a very wide distance, entire weekends end up dedicated to soccer, as opposed to the two to three hours or so required for a local recreational game. (Needless to say, this level of involvement probably only makes sense for players who are extremely passionate about the sport.)

To give you a clear picture of what you're getting into with whatever league option you're considering, this chapter tells you all about your various options, as well as some tips for how to choose between them. In any case, be sure to choose what works best for your family. Don't make a push for select soccer just because everyone else seems to be doing it. Let your child's interest level be your guide.

Which Team Should Your Child Play With?

When your child is getting started, this is a relatively easy question to answer for most families; simply sign up with the most convenient recreational team. As your child gains playing experience and becomes ready to move beyond the recreational level, your family will have some decisions to make.

Even when you are choosing that first recreational team, there are a few important considerations. Unless you live in a small or isolated community, you likely will have a choice between multiple youth soccer programs in your own or neighboring communities. If your family's activities all take place in one well-defined area, the choice will be fairly obvious. For many of today's families, however, it isn't that simple.

How much of a commitment is this?

The simple answer to this question is—however much time you want it to be. If you do not want to, or cannot commit much time to soccer, find a recreational program with limited practice time. For young recreational players, you'd be looking at a grand total of 2-3 hours per week for a couple of months at a time, twice per year. Older kids playing travel soccer will spend a bare minimum of 8 hours per week year-round, sometimes much more. Emotionally, there's a much longer commitment for travel soccer because the season lasts 8-11 months. Because recreational seasons last a mere 8 weeks or so, there isn't too much risk in giving it a try. If your family doesn't like it, you'll be done in a few weeks. Check out the details for each of the options in the *Comparing the League Options* table.

WHEN CHOOSING, YOU'LL WANT TO KEEP SEVERAL FACTORS IN MIND:

* *Quality of the program.* Not all youth programs are created equal. It is worth asking around to find one that will suit your family's needs and your child's temperament. Ask other parents at your child's school or colleagues at work about local programs. We'll talk a bit more later about exactly what constitutes a quality program, but for now start by finding out which programs other parents recommend.

* *Geography and convenience.* Remember that your child will need to get to practice at least once per week, as well as to one game per week. For ages 12 and above, there may be as many as three practices per week, plus games. Think carefully about the logistics involved. Your home town will not necessarily be the most conve-

nient league location. Where do you have the best carpool prospects? Can you make it from your work location to the practice fields by early evening?

* *Long-term effects on your social calendar.* You might think that you are simply picking a temporary recreational league just for the current season. As one of my Soccer Mom friends points out, however, the reality is that your child will quickly build strong relationships. Translation: You'll end up driving there a lot more often than just for practice. You'll also be driving there for play dates, sleepovers, and birthday parties. What's more, you may very well be driving there long after your child has moved on to another league. All else being equal, I recommend choosing a team close to your home and/or child's school. If you don't, you are setting yourself up for a lot of time in the car.

LEVELS OF PLAY

Once your child has a little bit of playing experience, you'll eventually need to make some decisions about the appropriate level of competition for your child's individual skills, playing goals and temperament. Contrary to what you might be led to believe on the sidelines, more competitive is not always better for every player. It is up to you to help guide your child in making the choice that is right for her as an individual.

Virtually every community youth soccer program offers at least two levels of play: recreational and select. Some communities (ours included) offer three levels: recreational, select, and travel. Players who make it as far as the travel team level will find themselves with a wealth of opportunities ranging from state to regional to national teams. But we're getting a little ahead of ourselves. Let's talk first about whether your child should play anything beyond recreational level.

The recreational vs. competitive decision sounds as if it might be a very difficult one, but for most families, the answer is obvious. If your child can't wait to get to practice, counts down the days to the next game, records all of the pro games on TV, and starts pick-up games with his buddies on non-practice days, he's clearly got a passion for the game that a recreational league won't satisfy in the long term. In my experience, a true passion for the game usually comes along with enough skill to make select soccer a good fit. (They are playing and thinking about the game constantly, after all!) On the other hand, some kids are much more excited about the social aspects of the team than about the game itself. They rarely think about soccer unless they are at an organized activity and don't go out of their way to improve their skills. And that's all just great, but they aren't likely to enjoy the more intense environment and time commitment required by select soccer. For these kids, continuing on with a recreational league and the relaxed environment it provides is the way to go.

Whichever way your family is leaning, be sure that you are choosing what is right for

Should She Specialize?

Before we move on, though, one consideration when choosing if and when to make the move to more competitive play has to do with the tricky question of sports specialization. Today's competitive club teams play nearly year-round. With the travel and training commitments, very few players manage to keep up meaningful participation in multiple sports for long after having taken this step up. Many experts argue against over specialization at too young an age. Even so, it is hard for both parents and children to let go of the fear that failing to specialize in their primary sport of choice will leave them behind the players who did specialize. While a detailed debate on how and when to specialize in a sport is beyond the scope of this book, I do want to raise it as an important consideration.

In the end the motivation needed to excel at the highest levels have to come from within the player. You can drive her to the games, but you cannot drive her to really play. She has to do that for herself.

your child. This is no time to succumb to peer pressure. The environment, time commitment, and cost are very different between the recreational and select paths. The remainder of this chapter will explore what you can expect at each level so that you can help your child choose her best path. To help you guide your player on the path that is right for him, I'll briefly discuss the key attributes of each type of team.

CLUB TEAMS

Each youth community, or club team, is run under the purview of a local soccer commission, which in turn operates within a state-wide soccer association. For example, our local youth soccer organization is called the Whatcom County Youth Soccer Association, and our state organization is called the Washington State Youth Soccer Association. Finally, the state organizations all operate within a national soccer organization. The largest two are U.S. Youth Soccer and U.S. Club Soccer. Both operate parallel nation-wide organizations for youth club soccer, and both are members of the U.S. Soccer Federation, which is the highest governing body for soccer in the United States.

Many clubs participate through both organizations. One of my sons' teams, for example, plays its regular season through U.S. Youth Soccer but participates in U.S. Club Soccer's regional and national championship series each summer. In January, they and other select teams in Washington State participate in the U.S. Youth Soccer Washington State Championship Cup tournament. Younger age groups now start their State Cup seasons in March in some areas. U.S. Youth Soccer organizes an analogous tournament in each state, as well as regional and national championships. U.S. Club Soccer, on the other hand, operates a parallel Regional and National Championship series each summer.

Recreational Teams

Recreational youth soccer teams are where virtually all young players will start their playing careers. To play on one of these teams, your child need only signup by the designated deadline and pay the appropriate registration fee. There are no try-outs, and no one is turned away for lack of skill or experience.

At the close of the registration period, a club registrar will divide all registered players into teams, assigning one or more coaches to each team. The exact process through which recreational teams are formed will differ from club to club. In some areas, the teams are simply randomized, while others attempt to group kids by geographic proximity. It is also common to keep kids who are returning from a previous season with the same team. When your player has been placed on a team, you will receive a call from the coach letting you know the time, date, and location of the first practice.

In a recreational league, the focus is placed squarely on fun. As you would expect, the environment is typically much less intense than on a select team—at least it should be. The cost and time commitments associated with these teams are also much less intense.

Recreational seasons typically cover just a couple of months per year, and practices are informal, short, and limited to twice per week. Travel during the regular league season is kept to a minimum, though older recreational teams might participate in a nearby off-season tournament or two. The coach is usually a friendly parent with an interest in soccer and a willingness to help out.

Sounds good, so what are the downsides? Well, none for some kids. The kids who just want to have fun with local friends in a low-commitment, low-pressure environment will find exactly what they are looking for in a recreational league.

SELECT TEAMS

For some kids, though, recreational soccer just doesn't provide enough runway to let their skills and passion for the game really take off. These kids may become frustrated by the lack of interest and dedication demonstrated by their teammates. Soccer is a team sport. As such, it eventually can become difficult for a stronger player to continue his or her development with-

Organization	Region	Role
FIFA fifa.com	International	The ultimate soccer authority. Governs international play, governs the rules of soccer, and organizes the World Cup.
U.S. Soccer Federation ussoccer.com	United States	This is the governing body of soccer in all its forms in the U.S., including all U.S. National Teams, U.S. World Cup Teams, and U.S. Olympic Teams
U.S. Youth Soccer (USYS) usyouthsoccer.org	U.S. Youth Soccer	Maintains a network of 55 state associations governing recreational and competitive soccer for youths ages 5-19. Programs are administered with the help of local coaches and volunteers.
U.S. Club Soccer usclubsoccer.org	U.S. Youth and Adult Soccer	U.S. Club Soccer is a non-profit organization committed to the support and development of competitive soccer clubs. U.S. Club Soccer supports the development of competitive and elite teams for age groups U12 and up and adults.
American Youth Soccer Organization (AYSO) soccer.org	U.S. Youth Soccer	AYSO's motto is "everyone plays." This nationwide grassroots program starts with a community-based league, called a region. Above that, AYSO divides the country into 14 geographic Sections based on player population.
Soccer Association for Youth (SAY) saysoccer.org	U.S. Youth Soccer	SAY is a recreational grass-roots organization with only five employees nationwide; it aims to keep fees low and provide opportunities for kids to play and have fun.

Which league are we in?

Confused? So am I, and my kids have been involved in these organizations for many years. Don't worry. Unless you are on the board of your local or state soccer association, you will not need to worry about whether your club is playing through U.S. Youth Soccer or U.S. Club Soccer. I mention all of this now only so that the names will sound familiar to you. Your state soccer association will choose its affiliation, and you will probably only see the implications of that choice in the form of specific association rules and regulations.

out teammates who are on a similar path; it is hard to fine-tune team passing skills when your teammates aren't making the right runs or sending the right passes.

These kids, too, are hungry for the soccer knowledge that comes from a qualified coach. Because truly knowledgeable, qualified coaches are too few and far between, they usually are recruited to coach the select teams. In short, if your child is passionate about soccer, he will most likely be happier in a select environment.

Teams within a select division may be tiered into A, B, and possibly even C teams (often delineated by colors, such as gold and silver, so as to make the hierarchy a little less obvious). The strongest 15-18 players will be placed onto the A team, with the next 15-18 strongest players being placed on the B team, and so on. All of these teams qualify as select because the players had to go through a try-out process. However, the A team will normally play in more competitive leagues and will travel more extensively than the other teams. In some cases, though, I've seen B teams that were very nearly competitive with the A team.

One thing to keep in mind is that team rosters can and do change from year to year. It is particularly common for kids to be shuffled between the A, B, and C select teams as they grow and develop. A player who may be maturing a little later than his teammates might not make the A team on the first go-round, but be a star in future years.

The goal when putting together a select team is to create a winning combination, rather than to preserve social ties. This means that your child may get separated from her buddies. If she is more into the social aspect of the team than the game itself, this may come as a crushing blow. On the other hand, if her primary passion is soccer, she may not mind finding a more challenging outlet at the cost of cramping her social style. My three boys all played select soccer (at varying levels of intensity), and all experienced getting separated from good friends. I'd like to be able to report that all of those friendships survived the separation intact. The truth is that some did and some didn't, but my opinion is that the relationships that drifted apart weren't that solid to begin with, so it is hard to say how much was lost.

TRAVEL TEAMS

Being chosen for a select team doesn't necessarily mean that your child will travel extensively. In our area, for example, we have a non-travel select program for 10 and 11 year olds, called a development league. It is intended to serve as a gentle transition between recreational and true travel soccer. The development league teams travel only within an hour or so of home, which allows them to experience a wider range of competition, while still keeping the travel to a minimum.

True travel teams can expect to cover much broader territory. The specific amount of traveling is all relative of course. On the Eastern Seaboard, teams can experience all of the competition they can handle within a relatively short geographic distance—say within two hours drive. In the western half of the U.S., with its lower population density and very large states, greater travel distances are required to reach the same level of competitive diversity. As a result, teams may occasionally travel three hours or greater each way for regular league games. In Washington, for example, the state's three most competitive leagues include teams from both eastern and western Washington. Once per season, we have to make the trip to Spokane, nearly six hours in each direction. For obvious reasons, most families turn this into a weekend-long outing. While these trips can be a lot of fun, they aren't cheap. Keep in mind that parents bear the cost of all travel, so participation on these teams can really add up.

COMPARING THE LEAGUE OPTIONS

Clearly there are significant differences between recreational, select, and school leagues (which we cover at the end of this section), and it is hard to keep them all straight. I've summarized the relative time and cost commitments you can expect in the table on the previous page. See Section 9, *Taking It to the Next Level* for a comparison of elite and college-level leagues. The costs provided here include league fees, equipment costs, tournament fees, and travel expenses. Please regard them as rough estimates. Don't take them too literally; instead, use them as a relative comparison.

The exact soccer calendar will vary with area of the country and level of play. You should consult your local league for the details in your area. The practice commitments listed here are based upon the recommendations of the U.S. Soccer Federation, as described in its excellent free e-book, *Best Practices for Coaching Soccer in the United States*. NOTE: In some locations, the seasons for girls' clubs have been moved from the traditional fall to spring in order to accommodate their high school schedules. While the months of the season may not match the table for girls, the overall length of the season should be approximately the same.

Comparing the League Options

Level of Play	Typical Season Calendar	In-Season Weekly Commitment	Travel and Tournaments	Cost
Recreational (U6-U7)	**Fall Season:** 8 weeks, September–October **Spring Season:** 8 weeks late March through early May	Practices: one or two per week, lasting 30–45 minutes each **Games:** one per week, lasting 20–30 minutes	None	<$150
Recreational (U8-U9)	**Fall Season:** 8 weeks, September–October **Spring Season:** 8 weeks, late March through early May	One to two practices per week, lasting 45–60 minutes each **Games:** one per week, lasting 30–40 minutes	No travel, rarely summer tournaments	<$200
Recreational (U10-U11)	**Fall Season:** 8 weeks, September–October **Spring Season:** 8 weeks, late March through early May	Two practices per week, lasting 60–90 minutes each **Games:** one per week, lasting 50 minutes.	No travel, one or two summer tournaments	<$200
Recreational (U12-U18)	**Fall Season:** 8 weeks, September–October **Spring Season:** 8 weeks, late March through early May	Two practices per week, lasting 60–90 minutes each **Games:** one per week, lasting 60–90 minutes	No travel, a few nearby, informal summer tournaments	<$200
Select (U10-U11)	**Fall Season:** 8 weeks, September–October **Spring Season:** 8 weeks, late March through early May	Two practices per week, lasting 60–90 minutes each **Games:** one per week, lasting 60–90 minutes	No travel, a few nearby, informal summer tournaments	<$300

Comparing the League Options

Level of Play	Typical Season Calendar	In-Season Weekly Commitment	Travel and Tournaments	Cost
Select (U12-U14)	**Fall League Season:** August–December **State Cup Season:** January–March **Summer Tournament Season:** May through August	Two to three practices per week, lasting 90–120 minutes each **Games:** one per week, lasting 60–80 minutes (tournaments will involve multiple games in a short period)	Possibly extensive travel within state. Several summer tournaments, usually within same state. One state or regional end-of-season tournament	<$2,000
Select (U15-U19)	**Fall League Season:** August–December **State Cup Season:** January–March **Summer Tournament Season:** May through August	Two to three practices per week, lasting 90–120 minutes each **Games:** one per week, lasting 80–90 minutes (tournaments will involve multiple games in a short period)	Possibly extensive travel within state, many summer tournaments, usually within their own multi-state region, one state or regional end-of-season tournament	$1,500-$5,000+ depending upon amount of travel.
Middle School	**One Season,** usually 6–8 weeks; note that the middle school season usually overlaps with the club season	Practices on every school day without a game **Games:** likely two per week, lasting 80–90 minutes	Travel is usually only to other schools within the same county, no championship tournament	<$100
High School	**One Season,** usually 6–8 weeks, plus district and state play-offs for successful teams. Usually in the fall for girls and in the spring for boys Note: HS season overlaps with the club season	Practices on every school day without a game, lasting 90–120 minutes **Games:** approximately two per week, lasting 80–90 minutes	Basic league travel is usually within county, at the end of each season there is an inter-district tournament, followed by state-wide tournament	<$100

TRYOUTS

Select soccer is a whole different ball game, so to speak. In addition to the obvious differences in terms of time commitment and cost, the fact that there are tryouts involved is game-changing enough.

The single biggest difference between recreational and select teams is the selection itself. Players cannot simply sign up for a select team. They must first participate in a tryout, which usually consists of one or two nerve-wracking playing sessions in front of a team of coaches whose job it is to rank players.

Each club runs tryouts in its own particular way, but almost all work by assigning players a number for use during tryouts in the hopes of removing any name recognition. Players usually are asked not to wear any clothing that mark them as having made a particular team previously. You should expect to sign a liability waiver and pay a small tryout fee to cover the costs of providing insurance for the day.

The tryout sessions themselves usually consist of a little bit of running and warming up followed by a series of short, small-sided games. Toward the end of the tryouts the coaches may put together teams for full-field scrimmages. Don't panic if you see your child on the sidelines during the later scrimmages. The selection coaches often will pull off kids that they have already decided to keep so that they can watch the ones they're not yet sure of.

Which brings up a last, but very important point; no matter how tempted you may be, please do not attempt to coach your child during tryouts. Not only does it embarrass your child, but it also annoys the coaches who have a hard enough time trying to no-

TIPS FOR STANDING OUT AT TRYOUTS

The more a player can draw positive attention to himself during tryouts, the better the chance of getting the coaches to take a fair look at his abilities. I've known a number of really good players who failed to get noticed during the critical tryout hours and were passed over. The selection coaches have a very difficult job. They are only human and have to rank dozens, if not hundreds, of kids, after watching them for a very short period; they are bound to miss a few gems. Here are a few common strategies for getting that all-important look:

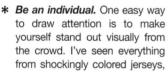

* **Be an individual.** One easy way to draw attention is to make yourself stand out visually from the crowd. I've seen everything from shockingly colored jerseys, to temporarily died purple hair to intentionally-mismatched socks.

* **Speak up.** The tryout is not the time to be shy. Using lots of positive verbal communication with other players on the field both draws attention and demonstrates an important skill. If a player is open, running for a pass, or has useful information for another player he should say so, and loudly enough to be heard.

* **Give 100 percent and then some.** This should go without saying, but surprisingly few kids remember how important it is to make a good first impression. If the player isn't willing to give it her all at tryouts, why should the coaches expect that to happen during games?

* **Play to your own level.** I've heard kids complain after tryouts that they couldn't look their best because they were put on a weak team during the small-sided games. While it is a little harder to stand out if you don't have anyone to help set up that beautiful give-and-go pass for you, the player shouldn't let this define her. Instead, she should go ahead and make the run, even if she knows that she's unlikely to get the pass. Similarly, she should make the through pass even if she's reasonably sure that no one will be there to receive it. The coaches are smart enough to see that the player is doing what she is supposed to be doing, even if she isn't getting any help.

tice subtle differences between dozens of kids. Stand back and let them enjoy playing—or better yet, take the time to take a stroll or get a coffee with your fellow Soccer Moms.

MAKING THE TEAM

When tryouts are over, you and your player are in for a nail-biting wait. Exactly how long you have to wait will depend upon the policies of your club. Some clubs use the rather unfortunate practice of publicly posting the final roster immediately after tryouts, or even worse, calling out names. While this does satisfy immediate curiosity, it also means that you'll have very excited kids standing next to very disappointed ones. They are just kids and probably don't have the emotional wherewithal to handle a situation like that gracefully. A better practice, in my opinion, is to send letters or post the results on the club website, so that each child can receive the information in privacy and have a chance to adjust.

IS THERE ANY HOPE OF MOVING UP IF YOU DON'T MAKE THE A TEAM AT FIRST?

Though there are cynical parents out there who may doubt me, the answer is yes—kids can and do move up in the select team hierarchy. With select teams starting as young as U11 in some areas, the first select team choice is being made between some pretty young kids. At the tender age of 10, a six month age difference can mean a world of difference in terms of physical strength and coordination. As a result, a kid who is on the older edge of the age spectrum or an early bloomer can temporarily look like a superstar, only to be surpassed as the other kids catch up in size and strength. It is for this very reason that all select team directors should do their best to go to tryouts with an open mind.

With that said, the reality is that getting a foot in the door early sure doesn't hurt anything. If the selection team already knows you, they are more likely to see you during next year's tryouts. And, because select teams usually train more and have access to better coaches and competition, kids on the less competitive teams probably will need to seek out additional training to avoid being left behind. All else being equal, if your child thinks that he may want to play select soccer, it is a good idea to try out for it the first year it is available. But if your child just isn't ready to play select soccer the first year it is offered, or if she is a late bloomer and simply doesn't make the first team, there is most definitely still hope for future years.

SCHOOL TEAMS

When I was growing up, playing for your school team was a big deal—at least on an equal par with club teams. Today, that is no longer the case. In fact, some competitive coaches argue that competitive players shouldn't waste time playing for their school teams.

If the sole purpose of participation in soccer was to obtain a college scholarship, then maybe, just maybe I could see their point. But there is a lot more to participation in soccer than the very slim chance of a scholarship and, therefore, some good reasons for players of all levels, both recreational and select, to consider playing for their school teams. The right choice for any given player, as with so much else that we'll discuss here, depends upon many individual factors.

MIDDLE SCHOOL

Much less intense than the high school team, middle school soccer still requires more commitment than your average after-school activity. Like high school soccer, there is generally either a game or a practice on most school days. Depending upon the size of the school, there will probably be tryouts. Most seem to try to accommodate as many kids as possible, however, by forming A, B, and possibly even C teams as necessary.

The season is short, lasting only six to eight weeks, and consists of playing other schools of roughly the same size from surrounding areas. Travel distances are limited for middle school soccer, and there usually isn't a post-season.

The level of play is generally somewhere between that of recreational and select clubs. The kids don't seem to mind that so much, because it is a chance for them to hang out with their friends. Not all kids can tolerate the daily practices at this age, especially when club practices are layered on as well. Among my three kids, for example, only one chose to play during all of his middle school years. The other two found that they didn't enjoy it enough to warrant the amount of time it occupied, preferring, instead, to stick just to their club teams and use the extra time to pursue other interests.

HIGH SCHOOL

Ask any mom who has had a child play for both a high school and a club soccer team, and she'll tell you that for reasons that are hard to describe, they are completely different animals. Where the club season is long and relatively evenly paced, the high school season is short and furious.

HIGH SCHOOL TRYOUTS

With the possible exception of very small high schools, there will always be tryouts. The top 15 to 18 kids will be placed on the varsity team, with the next 15 to 18 comprising a junior varsity (JV) team. Unlike club teams, placement on the varsity vs. junior varsity teams is not always strictly on ability. The player's year in school also can come into the decision. A senior, for example, who is even close in ability to a freshman, will usually get the nod to play on the varsity.

It is relatively uncommon for freshman boys to make a varsity team. Boys mature an amazing amount (physically anyway!) between their freshman and senior years. Girls, on the other hand, have generally reached their adult size and strength by early high school, making it much more common for freshman girls to make a varsity team than it is for freshman boys.

As with the middle school teams, my experience has been that the high school teams fall somewhere between recreational and select teams in terms of quality play. This isn't surprising when you consider that the top select teams draw from an entire metro area. Even if all of those kids chose to play high school—and they don't—there still would be some mix as they are parsed out between all of the high schools in the area.

Reunite With Friends

One advantage of high school soccer is that it provides an opportunity for kids on regional second-tier select teams, or even recreational teams, to get to play with their friends who play on the top-tier select teams. This adds an element of fun that often is overlooked as a benefit of participating in the high school season.

The High School Season

In our area, the main season starts in early March and continues through the end of April. Kids playing on club teams will find that the high school season starts immediately following the State Cup tournaments. For the last couple of years, my son's club team has had to report to high school practice the very next day after they finished State Cup play.

For middle- to lower-tier varsity teams and all JV teams, the end of the regular season in April is the end of the road. Top teams, however, will go on to a post season in May, which will progress through league, district, and state playoffs. If the team makes it past the league playoffs, the distances travelled become progressively longer, possibly even necessitating overnight stays.

What Do All Those Letters Mean?

Each state does it slightly differently, but most use a size ranking to avoid having large schools with their correspondingly large player pools compete against very small schools. You will see rankings from A (called single A) to AAAAA (five A). Though I've not come across them very often, I hear that there are size rankings even lower than single A, such as B.

The whole environment surrounding the high school season is very different from the environment for club soccer. For one thing, club games don't tend to draw crowds of fans the way high school games do, even though the club games usually are better soccer. A player who does well in club doesn't usually have a chance to show off for her peers until the high school season comes around. There tends to be a lot of energy and fun watching high school games, particularly for varsity teams. Last and perhaps not least, the high school games draw press coverage from local papers. It can be a really fun experience for the players to see their names and pictures in the paper.

Many games are played in high school stadiums under the lights, which adds to the excitement. Teammates from the select clubs get to have friendly rivalries when their respective high schools compete. All around, the high school season is fun for both parents and players.

PLAYERS: AGES AND ABILITY

One thing is for sure. The more your child plays soccer, the more he will learn and improve. Some kids, obviously, will improve faster than others, say if they are naturally more athletic, have seen older siblings play for years, or are lucky enough to get particularly skilled coaching. Still, there is a general progression that can roughly be tied to ages.

Keep in mind that, just like math, soccer skills are **cumulative.** Advanced concepts cannot be mastered unless basic techniques are already solid. The game is the sum of many connected fluid parts and cannot be taught in isolation. The only way to learn how to play soccer is, well, to play soccer.

Micro Soccer (U6-U7)

Little kids are a joy to watch. They aren't tied into winning or losing. They simply want to run around and have fun with their friends. The fact that they are doing so with a ball is almost incidental. Soccer at this age is often affectionately known as bunch ball because the kids are a long way from learning about specific positions or their relationship to other players. And that's the way it should be.

The goal for player development at this age group is to let them have as many opportunities as possible to touch the ball in relatively unstructured play. Along the way, they also will learn rough control of their bodies, balance, and social interaction. A U6 game can look like a lot of individual games that happen to all be taking place on the same field. That's OK. It really still is an individual thing at this age.

Since it is supposed to be about developing a personal relationship with the ball at this age, the players should be allowed to do just that. Parents and coaches shouldn't make a big deal about passing or sharing the ball. Just throw a ball out there, and let them go to it in whatever form works for them.

PRIMARY GRADES (U8-U11)

Hopefully, the joy of the earlier ages still will be apparent. Players usually will have mastered enough of the most basic skills that they can start to get a little bit of a feel for who belongs where on a field. Even so, there should be no emphasis on positional play, nor should there be any focus on winning or keeping score—though that's easier said than done. In my experience, kids will keep score and know who won, even if the adults don't. All players should get a chance to play different positions, and all should participate in both offensive and defensive play. Players should be encouraged to experiment, take risks and develop their own intuition for the game. Like the younger kids, they are still all about having fun. They are generally well-behaved, if a little rambunctious.

U12

By this age, you will start to see a divergence between players headed for competitive play and those who prefer to stay with recreational play. Especially with girls, you will start to see some dramatic differences in physical size and strength, which can lead to apparent inequities between abilities. Try to look past these, and remember that they are probably only temporary. Be sure to distinguish between soccer ability and simple advanced physical maturity. Don't write off that little player just yet. As long as she is given a chance to continue her development, she'll come along, quite possibly passing up that player who matured earlier.

The bodies of players at this age are getting geared up for puberty. The changes happening in their bodies may lead to annoying and sometimes painful conditions such as Osgood-Schlatter's and Sever's Disease, as skeletal systems stretch to keep up with the rapid growth. The rapid appearance of hormones on the scene means that players in this age group tend to tire easily. They also, as a gross generalization, tend to get a tad more argumentative at this stage.

Differences between boys' and girls' play

How do female soccer players differ from male soccer players? No, this is not the lead-in to a lame joke. Despite my firm belief in equality in general, I have to admit that there are significant differences. Girls, as a rule, do not respond well to criticism in front of a group, even if given constructively. The feedback will be taken much more positively if it is given in private. Boys, on the other hand, do not seem to mind so much if their feedback is given in public, especially if it is fair and constructive.

MIDDLE SCHOOL AGES

Players in the U12-U14 age groups (or perhaps slightly sooner for girls and slightly later for boys) will go through a period of rapid growth that often renders them less coordinated and agile than in their younger years. If they have had a good foundation in fundamental skills prior to this age, they will be able to make it through this rough period. Be patient with these players and understand that they will come back stronger and better after they get through this awkward phase.

This is where the transition to adult-style soccer should start to occur. Individual skills usually are developed enough, and the kids are able to comprehend more complicated positional play and development of strategy. It is the U14 age group in which the focus should start to transition from individual skills to include more talk of team issues.

HIGH SCHOOL AGES

During the high school years, players rapidly become bigger, stronger, and faster. You will see the speed of play increase dramatically. Those of you with multiple players will find that the play of the most talented middleschoolers is like watching high school in slow motion. This faster play requires players to develop the mental aspects of the game. The only way to stay in the game is to remain mentally tuned in at all times, ideally with plans in mind for each of the possible contingencies at the moment. The player should know where other players are and what he'll do ahead of time so that he can react quickly enough. The player should be updating his plans continuously as the play goes on. Soccer is a very mentally involved game at the older age groups.

3 Let's Play!

Now that you've got a feel for the breadth of league options available for your child, it is time to take a closer look at the game itself. This is the section that will explain—from a mom's perspective—what is going on out on the field. Turn to this section whenever you have a question about game-time action. Because very few Soccer Moms, even the very experienced ones, have ever had more than an anecdotal introduction to the rules, positional play, or strategy, there will be something in this section for just about all moms to learn (unless of course you referee on the side!).

Basic Skills: We'll start with a brief description of fundamental skills. Because there are many excellent how-to soccer skills books on the market, we won't spend a great deal of time rehashing these details. We'll assume for now that the coach is responsible for (and capable of) teaching these skills. We'll focus on providing you with the broad background you'll need to be able to recognize what your player is working on, why, and roughly what to look for so that you can provide your child with support at home.

Playing Positions: We'll then walk through soccer's basic playing positions. Like any group activity, soccer works best when participants are given specialized roles. This section will help you understand why your child is doing what he's doing. We'll also discuss why all of the positions are important, and what kinds of player strengths and temperaments best match which positions. Your player should be given the opportunity to try all positions regularly at least until the middle school years. Still, it is interesting to know what might be the best long-term match for her.

At the Game: Gametime is where all of the skills and positional play come together. In the *At the Game* section, we'll take a play-by-play look at what is happening during each segment of the game and, more important, why. By the end of that section, you should know what to expect, why everything goes down like it does, and what to look for.

Rules of Play: With a good understanding of the overall mechanics of the game in hand, we'll have a good framework for discussing the rules of play. This is the section that will help you to decipher why the referee is blowing the whistle and, just as important, why he isn't. You'll also understand what the referee means when he uses certain hand signals.

Basic Strategy: Finally, we'll discuss basic strategy, with emphasis on the word basic. Our goal is not to qualify you for a National A coaching license, but rather to give you a solid working knowledge of the game's strategies so that you can get more out of your many spectator hours. As with fundamental skills, even the most interested Soccer Mom probably doesn't care to understand all of the finer points of running a 4-3-3 formation with a flat back four. If you do, there are entire books dedicated to the subject. Please see the reference section for suggested reading. If you are happy with a solid working knowledge, we've got you covered here.

The Field: What are all of those markings, and what do they mean? I know this doesn't sound like a terribly interesting topic, but I bet there's something there that you might not have known before.

THE FUNDAMENTAL SKILLS

I keep saying how soccer has so many nuances and potential for lifelong learning. Even so, the basic required skills are relatively few in number. As your player is getting started, these are the skills she must learn.

It has often been said that the game is the best teacher. Most of the skills your child needs will naturally develop over the course of many practice sessions and games. She'll be given formal instruction as to proper technique; but far and away the best way to learn is to practice through a combination of free play, organized drills, and practice at home.

DRIBBLING

This most basic of soccer skills can be described simply as running with the ball at the player's foot. As the player runs, he will touch the ball lightly, usually with the instep, to move it just enough forward to keep up with the running pace. You might also hear this called carrying the ball—a term that is somewhat ironic, given that field players aren't allowed to use their hands at all. The ability to dribble is the most fundamental and arguably most important skill your child can learn. As he continues, he will need to learn to dribble at various speeds and be able to change direction with ease. Improvement in dribbling comes with time and practice.

Passing

Soccer is a team sport, which means, of course, that a player with the ball must be able to get the ball to a teammate from time to time. A player who can serve the ball to a teammate at the right speed and exactly to the player's foot is an important asset to his team. Players need to develop a sense for when they should pass the ball and when they should continue to dribble. The most common type of pass, especially

Dominant feet

Almost all players will have a dominant foot when they get started, but all should have the goal of cultivating competence with both feet as early as possible. The best way to do this is to consciously use the non-dominant foot often in training sessions.

for young players, is known as the push pass. In this type of pass, players will use the inside of their foot, swung as a pendulum from the hip, following through the pass in the direction that they intend the ball to travel. A properly executed push pass looks much like the leg is being used as a giant putter. As players grow in strength and ability, they will learn longer distance passes such as crosses.

TRAPPING

Trapping is the yin to passing's yang. This is the skill that allows a player to receive a ball and bring it under control. There are many types of traps. At the earliest levels, players will be taught to receive a pass by cushioning the impact with the inside of the foot (the same part of the foot, incidentally, used to execute the push pass). As players advance, they will add many more traps to their arsenal, including chest traps (bringing a ball down out of the air by cushioning it with the chest) and thigh traps.

SHOOTING

Without shooting, there can be no goals. The ability to take a good solid shot is highly prized. Depending upon the circumstances, a good shot will take different forms. In all cases, the quality of the resulting shot is largely the product of a proper foot plant on the non-kicking leg and solid connection and follow-through with the instep of the kicking leg.

HEADING

Heading is the technique for using the head to redirect a ball above waist level while it is still in the air. Thankfully, very young children don't have much occasion to head the ball and, therefore, get to avoid the headaches that typically accompany it for inexperienced players. As players get older and are more able to kick long passes with sufficient lift, the need to be a proficient header becomes more prominent. Proper technique involves using the flat part of the forehead to meet the ball. The force for the header should not come from the motion of the neck, but should instead come from a strong forward motion from the waist, with the neck held solid. Above all, players must remember that it is much better for you to head the ball than for the ball to hit your head.

Touch

Developing a good touch on the ball is an important part of the progression for any soccer player. A player with good touch is able to control the ball well in any circumstance. She can bring a trap down at her feet, dribble at speed, and place a pass with pinpoint accuracy. It is as if the ball has become an extension of the body. Good touch can only be developed by spending many hours with a ball on one's foot. Juggling, which can be practiced individually with only a soccer ball and a small amount of space, is considered the best drill for developing touch.

Vision

Like touch, vision is a component of soccer skill that will come only with time and practice. It refers to the ability to see the development of the play and thereby anticipate the movement of the other players. A player with good vision will know almost intuitively where space will open up, and how he can best react at the time.

DECISION MAKING

Each soccer game is filled with many individual decisions. With the possible exception of kick-offs and free kicks, nobody calls set plays during a game; there is no coach or quarterback to prescribe a player's next move. Instead, each and every player is truly left to his or her own devices during the heat of the game. Sure, there is lots of communication and discussion on the field—at least there should be—but in the end, each player must make his own decision about what to do and where to move during any given moment of the game. Soccer is fairly unique among team sports in this sense. The overall flow of the game is, therefore, created by the combined decisions of every player on the field. Those who have solid, and fast, decision-making skills will create a big advantage for their team.

BASIC PLAYING POSITIONS

One of the first things a new Soccer Mom should grasp is an understanding of the basic responsibilities associated with each of soccer's primary positions. Contrary to what you might be led to believe by watching the U6 set play in beehive formation, not all players on a field should be doing the same things.

In soccer there are four primary position types: ① goalkeeper, ② defender, ③ midfielder, and ④ forward. While there are any number of possible variations on how these positions are used and the team's overall formation, the basic characteristics of these positions have remained remarkably stable over soccer's long history and across teams and age divisions.

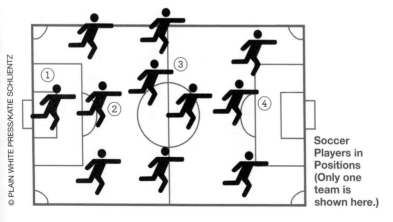

Soccer Players in Positions (Only one team is shown here.)

Position	AKA (also known as)	Key Objectives	Key Player Traits
Goal Keeper	Keeper	Defend the goal	Thick skin, fearless, comfortable making decisions, positive attitude
Defender	Center Back, Outside Back, Marking Back, Center D, and so on . . .	Primarily responsible for guarding the defensive third of the field	Good teamworker, calm under pressure, strong and confident, consistent
Midfielder	Middie, Mid	Coordinating the transition from defense to offense	Endurance, speedy, good vision, able to take decisive action, good touch on the ball and accurate passing skills
Forward	Center Forward, Striker, Outside Forward, Wing, Winger	Score goals	Aggressive, confident, super-competitive, crafty, opportunistic, good dribbler, speedy

GOALKEEPER

The goalkeeper, often abbreviated to keeper, is the brave defender of a team's goal. Take one look at a field, and you can see that a keeper is special. He must wear a uniform that distinguishes him visually from the rest of the team. He also is the lone player who is allowed to touch the ball with his hands, as long as he is within the confines of the penalty box. (Should the keeper accidentally handle the ball outside the penalty box, he will be issued a red card.) Technically, a keeper is allowed to roam wherever he wants on the field, but because it would leave the goal unprotected to do so, he usually stays put. I've never played keeper, other than the odd turns at a scrimmage, but I imagine that it must be as someone once described trench warfare—long periods of boredom punctuated by moments of sheer terror. Ok, maybe terror is too strong of a word, but you get the idea. The keeper's involvement in the game tends to stay at either extreme—either intensely involved or almost completely removed.

It isn't only the uniform that must be different in a keeper. She also must possess some distinctive personality traits to be successful. First and foremost, because the keeper usually is the last person who can stop the ball, she often is perceived as the player at fault if the ball makes it past her into the goal. You don't have to be a logistician to figure out that it had to have gone through ten of her teammates first and, therefore, is almost certainly a group problem. But that doesn't stop either the keeper or sometimes the teammates from placing blame on her. As a result, a thick skin is a prerequisite. On the flip side of this, when a keeper makes a big save, she can quickly become the team's hero.

Because the keeper often is called upon to organize the defense (she does have the best view of the field, after all), she should be comfortable making decisions, staying positive, and communicating with her teammates. She must also be able to keep a keen focus on the game, which can be really hard for young players when they've not touched the ball in a while. Physically, the best keepers are quick, decisive, and athletic. In older age groups, tall keepers have an advantage, but in younger age groups aggressiveness, confidence, and athleticism are more important than size.

Because it does require a bit more confidence and courage than do the field positions, it can sometimes be difficult to convince younger players to give goalkeeping a try. I personally think it is important for every player to get to have the experience from time to time during the younger playing years. You never can tell who is going to find that he loves the chance to be a hero and a team leader. If he doesn't get a chance to play, he will never know. I also think that teammates who've stood in the keeper's shoes before tend to be much less likely to criticize unfairly.

DEFENDERS

I was a defender for most of my playing career, and I wouldn't have had it any other way. The job of the defenders is to stop or at least slow down the opposing team's attack until the team can get more numbers (more players) back to help out. While they can range forward and become part of the team's attack for brief periods, defenders primarily occupy the defensive third of the field.

Defenders have responsibilities. No matter which defensive system the team is using (and there are many), the fact remains that defenders are responsible for guarding either specific players or specific areas. As a result, playing as a defender can feel a little more constrained, almost as if you are playing on a leash. Because defenders must work together to be effective, they must be able to enjoy working with and supporting other players. In other words, they must be more concerned with team performance than looking good themselves. Like goalkeepers, defenders can be easily blamed when something goes wrong, albeit to a lesser extent. They too, must have somewhat thick skins and the ability to avoid panic when under pressure from the opposing team. Finally, the team depends upon defenders to be strong, consistent, solid players.

How do I explain that defense is a good position?

ALL positions are important on a team. Try reminding your child that preventing the other team from scoring is every bit as important as helping your own team to score. After all, there is much truth to the old adage that the best offense is a good defense. Not every player has what it takes to be a defender. If your child does, it should be seen as an honor, not a punishment. Finally, point out that defenders get many chances to be the hero by making a dramatic save at a critical moment.

Defenders come in two primary varieties: center backs and outside backs, also known as marking backs. Center backs are responsible for anchoring the critical area in front of the goal and may or may not be marking individual players. Because they often help to organize the defense by sorting out which defender should be marking which player, a good center back will have good vision and will be a strong communicator. Later, when players are old enough to be sending long crosses past the goal mouth, it is helpful if a center back is tall enough to rise above the crowd and head the ball out of danger. Which brings me to another point; center backs should be comfortable heading the ball.

Outside, or marking, backs work toward funneling players away from the goal's mouth. Their job is to break up and slow down the progress of the offense. Increasingly, outside backs are asked to participate in offensive plays by making long overlapping runs to receive a ball from a midfielder.

MIDFIELDERS

Midfielders, also called middies, are the workhorses of the team. I've heard it estimated that a midfielder playing on a full-size field will run somewhere in the neighborhood of six to eight miles in the course of a single game. What's more, they are dragging a ball along with them for part of that distance. Obviously, they must be fit and prepared to work hard during a game.

Situated as they are in the middle of the field, midfielders are responsible for coordinating the transition from defense to offense. Because this transition is so critical to the game's ultimate outcome, it has been said that games are won or lost in the midfield. (Perhaps that would be a good thing to mention to any midfielder who happens to blame a loss on the defense?) The primary territory of a midfielder is exactly what you'd expect from the name—in the middle third of the field. However, because they are called upon to support both offensive and defensive plays, it is no wonder that midfielders cover so much territory.

In order to best serve the role as coordinators of the transition between defensive and offensive modes, midfielders should be fit, well-rounded players who are quick on their feet and have good vision. They usually have to make quick decisions under pressure, so they should be able to quickly assess the development of play and take decisive action. In addition, because the best offensive plays often begin with a perfect pass sent up to the forwards from the midfield, midfielders also should possess a good touch on the ball.

As with defenders, the specific nature of the midfielder's role depends upon whether they are positioned in the center or on the outside of the field. Center midfielders must be particularly adept at reading the development of play. They need to anticipate where their forwards will be moving to serve them the perfect pass. When the opposing team takes possession of the ball they must similarly anticipate the movement of their players so that they can take action to break up the play be-

Why can't everyone be a forward?

To draw an analogy from that other football game, having everyone play forward would be like having no defensive squad to send out when the opposing team lines up for the snap. The soccer field is rather large and it takes the whole team to cover it properly. Sure, forwards play an important part, but they are simply the finishing touch to the important work of the team as a whole. Without the actions of the other players, there is nothing to finish. And without being able to defend your goal, there is no way to win. Finally, not everyone even wants to be a forward. I've said it before, but I'll say it again—all positions are equally important.

fore it develops into a dangerous scoring opportunity. Outside midfielders tend to perform long overlapping runs. They often use long crosses to send a forward on an offensive run. Outside midfielders are often asked to stay wide to help the team make use of the field's full space.

FORWARDS

As a group, forwards have one and only one task—to score goals. Unlike the defenders who can often feel restrained by their responsibility to react to others, forwards are free to roam in unpredictable patterns that are designed to confuse their defenders. As with the other positions, the best forwards tend to have certain dominant personality traits. You often will hear good forwards described as aggressive, confident, super-competitive, crafty, and opportunistic. Physically, forwards should be fast and extremely talented dribblers. Because they have to react quickly in order to pounce on each scoring opportunity, they often have to go on well-honed instinct, using excellent touch to get a shot off.

Center forwards, also called strikers, usually are the highest scorers on the team. And for good reason—they serve as targets for the entire team. The very purpose of the team's offensive thrust is to eventually get the ball to the striker, whose job it is then to turn and shoot. It is common for strikers to receive long balls in the air. Therefore, the most effective strikers are able to use their heads to redirect a ball past the keeper. Those long balls that can't be headed in have to be brought down to the foot and shot, which of course means that strikers have to have very strong trapping skills. It is often helpful for strikers to be tall and physically solid enough that they aren't easily pushed off the ball by defenders.

Outside forwards, called wings or wingers, are primarily charged with making long runs down the side to receive a ball

The Captain

While not an official position, the role of team captain is, nevertheless, an important one. Typically awarded to a player who has demonstrated leadership in one form or another, the captain's primary role is to serve as a team leader during a game. Sometimes the captain is designated by the coach and sometimes by a vote of players. Sometimes a player will be made captain for the year, whereas other teams will rotate captains on a week-by-week basis.

During a game, the captain is often marked by a special arm band. However chosen and for whatever period, a team's captain has certain responsibilities on game day. First, he must represent his team in the coin toss before the game. He also is the player designated to communicate with the referee on behalf of his team. If any player has a grievance to discuss with the referee, it is supposed to go through the captain. The captain will also, though not always, lead his team in warm-ups prior to the game. In any case, being designated as a captain is a sign of honor and respect.

from the midfield. They should stay wide to provide an outlet for the midfield and defense under pressure. Once she receives the ball, the winger's job is to keep possession of the ball and penetrate into the opposing team's defensive third. At the right moment, the winger will combine with the other forward(s) to create a scoring opportunity. She may slide an accurate pass into the striker for finishing or decide it is better to pass back to a midfielder or to cross the ball to the winger on the opposite side. Though they do regularly score goals, outside forwards don't tend to score as often as strikers. Instead, they rack up goal assists (which, if you ask me, are every bit as important). Wingers share many characteristics with outside midfielders. For this reason, it is very common that the same player will fit well into either position.

AT THE GAME

With all of the basics out of the way, we can get down to the crux of the matter. What can you expect to happen on game day? What does it all mean? How can you best enjoy it and help your player to enjoy it as well?

Once you know what to look for, you'll see that all games, across all leagues and age groups, are made up of very predictable components. This section will provide a guided tour of the game, from the warm-up all the way through post-game activities.

INTELLIGENT SPECTATING

Before we get too deep into describing exactly what will happen on game day, I'd like to say a few words about being a more intelligent observer of the game. Soccer is a game of enormous creativity and fluidity. It is comprised of a series of innumerable individual decisions that together create a full picture of the game. When you watch your next game, try this little experiment. As each movement of the ball takes place, try thinking along with the players. Pick any player and ask yourself what her choices are at any given moment—there will be many. Watch how she reacts and the associated impacts on the flow of the game. My own opinion is that too many kids have been given the idea that in situation X, they must always do Y. That simply isn't true and, worse, it takes credit away from the creativity and decision-making skills that kids are exhibiting as they play. Very few spectators take the time to stop and appreciate the game at this level. I think you'll find it much more interesting if you do.

What kinds of decisions should you watch for? There are many. If a player happens to have the ball, he will have to decide whether to pass or to keep the ball. If he decides to pass, to whom should he pass? If he decides to keep it, does he take on the opposing player or post up and wait for additional options to open up? If he doesn't have the ball, he will have to consider whether to track with an opposing team member or to make a run into space in order to create an option for a teammate. He also will have to determine whether to try to get the ball back now or to wait for a more opportune time.

It is because there are so many decisions to be made in an instant that coaching from the sidelines simply doesn't work. Players have to be exposed to these situations in practice so that they can develop their own intuition for the right action in any situation.

Who knew they were learning critical thinking along with physical skills?

What to look for if you can't understand the rules

As you're first learning to watch and enjoy your child's game, don't worry if you don't understand everything that is going on at every moment. Notice how the players are trying to work together toward—quite literally—a common goal. Watch how they support each other as they move forward and as they defend against the

other team. Appreciate the skill that they are displaying. Don't worry, as you learn more about the game, you'll have much more to appreciate and enjoy. For now, focus on watching your child have fun getting exercise with her friends.

Anatomy of a Soccer Game

No matter the level or age group, there is a certain ritual that accompanies a soccer game. Here's an insider's look at who is doing what, when, and why on game day.

Warm-up

Players will be asked to arrive prior to kick-off time to allow the team to get organized and warmed up. For very young kids, it may be only 20 or 30 minutes, whereas older kids will be asked to arrive 45 minutes to an hour ahead of game time. Each team will develop its own warm-up routine. When the kids are very young, the warm-up routine will be led by a coach. By the time players are 11 or so, the warm-up routine can be led by a captain. You'll see them start out with a slow jog, perhaps some stretches, followed by a series of quick shooting drills. The keeper usually is warmed up by having a coach or designated player take shots on the keeper in rapid succession.

Coin toss

Just before the appointed kick-off time, the referee will signal for the captains to join him in the center circle for a coin toss. The winner of the toss gets to choose which half to defend. The usual strategy is to choose the least favorable position in the first half in order to have the advantage for the second half—unless of course the conditions are expected to change for the second half. What constitutes an advantage? Wind direction and sun, primarily. If the playing field is at all not level or muddy in spots, that will be taken into consideration. Generally, the coach already will have instructed the captain which side to choose. The team losing the coin toss will kick off. After the coin toss, some referees will call all players to the center line for an equipment check. This used to be a very common practice, but I've not seen it recently.

KICK-OFF

After the conclusion of the coin toss, teams will gather by the coach, who will quickly give last-minute instructions regarding the line-up or game strategy. After a brief cheer (possibly for boys, probably for girls), the starting players will run out onto the field to take their assigned positions. Each team must line up on the half of the field they are defending. The ball is placed at the very center of the center circle. Only players from the team kicking off are allowed within the circle. To officially kick off, a player must simply kick the ball forward. Any kick to any player, near or far, is allowed, as long as the ball goes forward. The original kicker cannot touch the ball again until at least

Why do the defenders just stand there?

At first glance, it might appear that defenders are just standing around enjoying the sunshine. They aren't. (Well, at least they shouldn't be.) They are, instead, maintaining proper position in readiness for the next attack. If all players were to be an active part of every attack, there would be no one left back on defense to deal with the counterattack when it inevitably occurs. This isn't to say that defenders get to tune out and take a break. They should be constantly watching the development of the play to anticipate a counterattack and constantly adjusting their position accordingly.

one other player has touched it. And, yes, it is allowable to score a goal directly from a kick-off. It's obviously really tricky and, therefore, almost never happens, but still fun to think about!

FIRST-HALF PLAY

Finally, the part we've all been waiting for. Once the ball has been kicked off, play will continue on for the allotted time plus any stoppage time, with the fans cheering (hopefully) positive things all the while. Along the way, the game will be stopped only for a goal, a ball that has gone out of bounds, a foul, or an injury. OK, maybe that's not strictly true. The referee can stop play for just about anything she wants—it just doesn't happen very often outside the above-mentioned reasons. If say, an alien ship were to land on the field, I would imagine that the game would be stopped then too. I'll let you know if I ever see that happen.

HALF TIME

When the referee has determined that the official time has expired, he will blow two whistles (one medium blast followed by one long blast) and point his arm toward the center circle indicating the end of the half. Each team will retreat to its own bench for a rest period of approximately 15 minutes. FIFA rules say that a half-time interval must not exceed 15 minutes. Many younger age groups will have a shorter half-time interval of more like 10 minutes. During this time, players will get a brief rest, something to drink, and a short talk from the coach, who should review strategy, provide a few quick pointers and, hopefully, some encouragement. The referee will return to the center circle and clearly signal when it is time to restart the game.

WHAT IS THE COACH SAYING?

You'll hear a lot of talk during the game from most coaches—hopefully, all of it positive and constructive direction for the players. In my opinion, the very best coaches don't chatter constantly during the game. They know that the time for lengthy instruction is during training. Still, a concise and timely bit of advice or encouragement can sometimes make all the difference. Here's how to translate some of the most common soccer-specific phrases you might hear from your child's coach.

* **Find space.** Run into an area of the field that is less densely populated in order to either receive a pass or to force a defender out of position.

* **Show yourself.** Move out from behind an opposing team member to become a reasonable pass option.

* **Find feet.** A gentle reminder that passes should be given to teammates where they make use of them, at their feet. Usually said when passes haven't been on target.

* **Support.** A reminder to players without the ball to move into positions that either (a) provide their teammates with pass options or (b) provide a backup option in case an offender manages to get past them.

* **Use your teammates.** A perhaps gentler version of "PASS!"

* **One of you.** Said when two or more players are going for the same ball or are covering the same player.

* **You've got drop.** Used to let the player with the ball know that they have a pass option available behind them. You'll hear players say this often during a game as well.

* **Possession.** An admonition to focus on safely keeping control of the ball as opposed to aggressively trying to further the attack. This advice usually comes up if the coach wants players to play conservatively toward the end of the game in order to preserve a lead.

* **Push up.** Usually directed at the defense, this phrase reminds players to move forward to take advantage of the offside rule with the idea of preventing the offense from having too much space in which to get an attack organized.

* **Get back.** Drop back into a defensive position. Note that this can be relevant for all players, even forwards. It is most often directed at midfielders who've made an offensive push, but who now have to get back to help out on defense once possession has changed.

* **Talk.** A reminder to all players that they need to work more on communicating with their teammates.

* **Patience.** Almost always directed at a player in a one-on-one defending situation, this is a reminder to avoid making a risky attempt to take a ball away from the offensive player but to instead wait until the offensive player makes a mistake or until the defensive player has back-up.

* **Go to ball.** The opposite of patience, this is a directive to make an immediate attempt to get possession of the ball.

* **Mark up or find your mark.** Find a player from the opposite team to defend. You'll hear this most often in restart situations like throw-ins, corner kicks or free kicks.

* **Goalside.** A reminder for a defender to position himself between the offensive player and the goal. It sounds obvious enough, but you'd be surprised at how often players, especially young ones, need this reminder.

* **Carry it.** Keep dribbling the ball for a moment longer.

* **Go to goal.** An encouragement for an offensive player to make a drive directly to the goal.

* **Have it or hit it.** Take a shot on goal!

* **Unlucky.** A polite and concise way of saying, "Well, what you just tried to do didn't work out, but it was a good try."

* **Well-in.** Congratulations on a good tackle or other attempt to go in for a 50-50 ball (i.e. a ball not currently in either team's possession).

Second-half kick-off and play

Procedures for starting up and playing the second half are identical to what you saw in the first half, with one exception —players will line up to defend the opposite goal to what was defended the first time. When the allotted time plus stoppage time has passed, the referee will indicate the end of regulation play by blowing three whistle blasts (two medium and one long) and pointing to the center circle.

Why you should be excited by a 1-1 result

Though it might seem frustrating to players and spectators at times, there are actually some upsides to a tie game. For one thing, an even score usually means that the teams were well matched, providing a healthy challenge for *both* sides. Even better, with a score of 1-1 both teams have had a chance to experience the success of a goal, and spectators have had something to cheer about.

Post game

When the game is officially over, each team will return to its respective bench. It is traditional for the coach to speak a few short words to her players, lead the team in a short post-game cheer (something along the lines of "good game!"), then lead the players into the post-game handshakes. To do this, each team forms a single-file line and approaches the center circle from its respective benches. The coaches usually are the last in line. Players shake hands and say "good game" or something like it to each opposing player and coach in turn. The referees usually are standing off to the side and are thanked with handshakes following the team handshakes. After all the shaking is done, teams usually gather for a longer post-game talk from the coach. Among very young kids, there also may be a post-game snack distributed. I'm not a fan of this practice myself, but it is common.

Who is Where and Why

As the team prepares to line up for kick-off, you'll see the players take up precise positions on the field, depending upon the formation or system of play they are using. The team with the kick-off will have two players within the center circle. All other players must remain outside the center circle. The referee also will take her place outside the center circle on the center line. It is her job to make sure that each team has the right number of players on their respective halves of the field (and no one on the other half!) before kicking off. Each assistant referee, more commonly known as an AR, will position himself approximately level with the last defender on his designated half. Coaches usually will be on opposite sides of the field, and non-starting players will be in a designated bench area, whether or not there is an actual bench involved. Once the kick-off whistle blows, of course, any participant could be anywhere at any time!

Stoppage time

Despite soccer's wonderful continuous play, there still can be significant time when the play has been stopped for one reason or another. This is called stoppage time. If your team is down 1-0 and the clock is running out, there's no need to panic over the seconds ticking away while an injury is attended to.

Panicking over the injury may be warranted, but don't panic over the time. The referee is required to approximate the amount of time associated with play stoppage and add it back to the standard play time at the end of the half. So, if the game was supposed to have 30-minute halves, but the referee has estimated four minutes of stoppage time, the play will continue for 34 minutes. And don't bother arguing. The referee, and the referee *only*, can determine how much stoppage time is appropriate. So there.

Why isn't my child running to the ball?

She probably isn't supposed to. Only one player can control the ball at a time. If everyone runs to the ball at once, there is no one left to pass to, and there is no one left to defend against opposing players. The game turns into a disorganized mess. There are many important roles to fill *off-ball* as well. For example, your child may be running to empty space in order to spread out the defenders or receive a pass, or she may be keeping tabs on an opposing player. In short, savvy spectators know that there is a lot of important action going on in a game that isn't directly associated with running on to the ball.

STARTING AND NOT-STARTING (SUBSTITUTION AND PLAYING TIME)

Because soccer is a tiring sport, each team will carry more players on the roster than are allowed on the field at any one time. (Try running around for 60 to 90 minutes, and you'll understand why!) This practice allows for the coach to give weary players a rest using substitution, the process of replacing one player with another during the game. Rules for substitution vary by league. In all cases, substitution only can take place during a stoppage in play (for example, if the ball has gone out of bounds). The only question is on which stoppages are substitution allowed. Most recreational leagues allow substitution on any stoppage. Other leagues may only allow substitutions when the substituting team is awarded possession of the ball upon restart after the stoppage.

The players on the field at the time of the kick-off are referred to as starters. The remaining players on the team for that game are called the substitutes or more commonly, subs. In recreational soccer, experts recommend that all players play equally. This makes sense since the emphasis for recreational soccer is supposed to be on fun and player development, rather than on winning. In other words, stronger players should get no preference, simply by virtue of their skill. The net effect is that the starters and subs will rotate on a game-by-game basis.

On a competitive team, especially U14 and younger, the focus should still be on player development and, therefore, many experts recommend that all players get equal time there too. On many teams, however, that's not what happens. Because there is pressure from many quarters to win, the strongest players get to start and get more than their fair share of time. Earning a starting spot is a badge of honor. Unfortunately, too many teams settle on starters at the beginning of the season.

In my opinion, a better approach is for the coach to set the starting lineup based on who is playing best right now. This constant source of competition helps lift the level of the entire team. The starters can't become complacent, and the subs have incentive to continue improving because they have a realistic chance of moving up to a starting spot for any given game.

I am also of the opinion that it serves both the team and the individual development of players to ensure that subs all get substantial playing time. The only way to truly develop players is to give them playing time, and lots of it. And, because you never know when a starter will get hurt, change sports, or change teams, having a deep team with strong, well-developed substitutes is better for everyone. Of course, this only applies for teams that are not assigning starting time equally.

Why is my kid riding the bench?

If your child is a perennial sub, encourage him to keep heart, keep trying, and improve his skills. As players grow and mature, there can be a lot of shifting between who is the strongest and most skilled at any one time. On my sons' teams, I've watched players who used to be substitutes not only become starters, but become team stars. By the same token, starters should not get complacent, because others will be along to challenge them soon enough.

RULES OF PLAY

You'll have a much better time watching the game if you understand its rules. In any game, part of the fun is figuring out how to work with and take advantage of the rules.

The good news is that soccer's rules are relatively few, and with the exception of the dreaded offside rule, the most important aspects are simple to understand. The bad news is that I often am shocked at how many long-time soccer fans are misinformed. And since we're going to be talking about formal rules, we ought also to call them by their proper name: the Laws of the Game.

Each league and even age level is free to vary the Laws of the Game to suit their own needs. However, every organization I know of strongly bases their laws on the Laws of the Game, produced by FIFA. This publication is freely available in PDF format at *http://www.fifa.com/worldfootball/lawsofthegame.html*. I highly encourage everyone who is involved in soccer in any form—playing, parenting, spectating, coaching, or refereeing—to have a look at this excellent document. It is a whole lot more readable than you would think. Because the FIFA rules are at the core of local laws everywhere, I'll use those as the basis here.

THE REFEREE IS IN CHARGE OF THE LAWS

Keep in mind, though, that the interpretation of the Laws of the Game is best left to experienced and well-trained referees. In fact, a large portion of the Laws of the Game document is dedicated to interpretation of the rules in various situations. Each time the Laws are revised, FIFA's International Football Association Board meets to discuss and further clarify the rules. Clearly, they aren't black and white, and there is a lot that goes into calling them correctly.

So please do try to keep all of this in mind the next time you are tempted to question a referee's call, particularly if you've never taken the time to study FIFA's Laws of the Game yourself. Here's the thing: Very few players, parents or coaches actually read the Laws directly. Take me as an example. I've been involved with soccer in one form or another for more than 35 years now, as player, coach, and parent. I considered myself very familiar with the rules. Yet, other than looking up a few specific situations here and there, I had never read the Laws in their entirety until I was researching this book. Having now thoroughly read the Laws, I can say that there are many subtleties and gray areas. I can't tell you how many times I've seen parents and even coaches yelling at the ref until they were blue in the face about a *bad call,* when the call was actually correct, but related to a little-known part of the law. Besides, if you are a parent, coach, or other biased spectator, you will be predisposed to see things in a light most favorable to your own team. It is simple human nature.

Scoring

The rules for scoring in soccer are as simple as can be. A goal will be awarded to a team if the ball has crossed all the way over the goal line in the goal defended by the other team. By all the way over, I mean that no part of the ball is still touching the line. Notice that I didn't say anything about who caused the ball to go into the goal. It doesn't matter. If a ball goes into the goal defended by the other team, your team will be awarded a goal. Unless, that is, a foul occurred during the play that resulted in the goal. Whoever has the most points at the end of the game wins. See, it really is a beautifully simple game.

*O*VERTIME

If the game is a draw as of the end of regulation time, there may be an overtime session.

DECIDING A GAME BY PENALTY KICKS

To decide a game by penalty kicks (PKs), each team much choose five players to take kicks. Only players who were on the field at the end of the previous period are eligible. You might see a coach making frantic last-minute substitutions for this very purpose. The poor goal-keeper lines up on the goal line as if it were a firing line. And to some extent, it is. There is an old saying that goalkeepers don't save penalty kicks, forwards miss them. In other words, the odds are firmly with the kicker. Goalkeepers aren't allowed to move off of the line until the ball has been kicked. Once players can kick strongly enough, all a keeper can do is guess and dive.

If there is one thing you can say about PKs, it is that there is a lot of drama involved. All 10 of the chosen kickers will be asked to remain within the center circle. Meanwhile, the referee will walk the two keepers down to the chosen goal. The first keeper (chosen by a coin toss) will be positioned at the center of the goal line, and the referee will call the first kicker forward. I always pity the kickers as they make the long walk from mid-field to the penalty spot, all eyes on them, knowing that it is their shot to miss. When the referee blows the whistle, the player must take his shot. If the keeper has moved early, or the kicker has kicked before the referee signaled his permission, the kick will not stand and must be retaken.

This little drama will play out rotating between teams until either one team has outscored the other, or the first group of five shooters from each team has been exhausted. If the score is tied at the end of the first group, kicks will continue one by one, rotating between teams, in the same order, until one team has scored one more goal than the other. If the game remains undecided after every field player has taken a kick, the first players will take a second kick. The longest streak of PKs I've heard of was 12 each in a state high school play-off game last year.

WHO IS THE REFEREE AND HOW IS HE TRAINED?

The referee is one of the unsung heroes of the game. She must wear many hats, and often with little thanks from the participants.

The referee is in charge of making sure that a game is played fairly, safely, and in accordance with the Laws of the Game. She must also manage logistical details like tracking time, keeping score and recording bookable offenses (yellow and red cards). Ideally, she is independent of connections to either team, though practical considerations may make this impossible from time to time.

You'd never know it judging from the enthusiasm with which some spectators and coaches argue, but when it comes to decisions related to the game, the authority of the referee is absolute. Yell all you want, but nothing will come of it; soccer contains no provision for appeals and on-field decisions are never changed.

With all that they have to think about, it is no wonder that high-level referees receive a great deal of training over their careers. Obviously though, they have to start somewhere. After completing an initial 16-hour course, new referees will usually earn their stripes by refereeing for very young, recreational games where knowledge of the game's subtleties isn't needed and where small officiating mistakes aren't likely to ruin anyone's season. As they gain experience and complete additional courses, referees are allowed to officiate for older ages and at higher levels of competition.

WHAT'S GOING ON WHEN THE REF BLOWS THE WHISTLE?

Soccer games are noisy. You'll hear players saying all kinds of things to coordinate play (the vast majority of which, hopefully, are printable here). You'll hear fans yelling. (We can hope its a positive refrain.) But above all, you'll hear lots of whistles. What causes a referee to whistle, and what do his gestures mean? We'll find out in this section.

STARTING AND CONCLUDING THE HALVES

The very first official sound that you will hear is the referee's whistle indicating the official start of the game. Once all players are lined up and the referee has made her final checks, she will give one long whistle blast to indicate that the attacking team may kick-off. Two whistles (one short, one long) will indicate the conclusion of the first half, and three whistles (two short and one long) will indicate the conclusion of regulation time. In between, you'll hear many other single whistles indicating fouls or other forms of game stoppage.

The Ball is Out of bounds

Game play will continue only as long as the ball stays within the field of play. The ball is considered to be within the field of play if any part of the ball is still touching any part of the line (or vertical plane created by the line for balls in the air, to be technically correct). What happens after the ball goes out of bounds both depend upon where it went out and who was the last to touch it. In every case, the assistant referee and referee must make a decision as to the type of restart to be awarded and to which team it should be awarded. The latter question is simple to describe, but harder to answer. In all cases, the restart should be awarded to the opponent of the team who last touched the ball (even if the player didn't mean to touch it—you'll see players intentionally kick the ball off of their opponent in order to get a throw in, but we're getting ahead of ourselves). However, that's often easier said than done. As I'll say probably a hundred times during this book, the ref and AR are only human. The action is often fast and the view obscured. They'll do the best they can, but they won't always get it right.

Throw-in. The most common restart situation by far is the throw in. Whenever a ball goes out of bounds, a throw-in will be awarded to the opponent of the last player to touch the ball, whether intentional or not. For many years, throw-ins were simple to execute, and all looked the same. In the past several years, there has been a new trend toward throw-ins that look more like they belong in a gymnastics competition than a soccer game. Because all of the strength of a throw-in comes from

HOW TO FLAG

At the recreational level, parents are often called to help out as an assistant referee, also known as a flagman. If you get roped into this job, it shouldn't cause you too much stress. It is pretty easy to do. And you need not worry too much about making a mistake. You will just be making recommendations to the referee, who has the responsibility of making the official call.

Your duties are pretty simple. You and a counterpart across the field will each be responsible for one touch-line and for one half of the field. You will be given a flag to indicate to the referee what you see in these situations:

* **When the ball has crossed the touchline on your side of the field.** (Remember that the ball is not considered to be out of the field of play unless it is completely over the line.) You will indicate that the ball is out, as well as which team should receive the ball upon restart, by pointing your flag in toward the goal at which the team in question is shooting.

* **When the ball has crossed the goal line on your half of the field, but is not a goal.** If the attacking team was the last to touch the ball, indicate that a goal kick should be awarded by pointing to the corner of the goal box. If the defending team was the last to touch the ball, then you should indicate that a corner kick should be awarded by pointing to the corner flag.

* **When you see a violation of the offside law in your half of the field (assuming you're helping out for a game with the offside rule in effect—it won't be if very young kids are playing).** To communicate this to the referee, you should run to the point on your touchline that is level with the location of the offense, stand with both feet together and the flag raised high overhead. But in any case, just remember to do your best. The referee will simply overrule you if he thinks you've made a mistake.

* **When you see any foul that has occurred where you've got a better view than the referee.** Indicate this by simply raising your flag.

* **If, during a penalty kick, you see the goalkeeper move off of the goal line before the ball has been kicked.** If you see this happen, raise your flag.

THROW-IN RULES

Your basic throw-in is very simple. Players can do almost anything as long as it doesn't violate these basic rules:

❋ The ball must be thrown in from the same point it left the field. Don't be surprised if the thrower cheats up a little toward the opposing goal.

❋ The thrower must keep both feet outside the field of play (touching the line is OK), and both feet must be on the ground when the ball is thrown.

❋ The thrower must use both hands, and the throw must start behind his head and proceed straight over it (no twisting or turning allowed).

❋ After the throw, the thrower cannot touch the ball again until another player (from either team) has touched it.

❋ All other players must stay at least two meters away from the thrower until the ball has been thrown. This is a little known rule, because it is so rarely enforced. But it is on the rule books, so there you go.

Not that it comes up very often, but even if a player could throw the ball directly into goal, it would not be allowed; you can't score directly from a throw-in. There also is no such thing as offside on a throw-in.

What happens if these rules are broken? If the thrower touches the ball again before another player, an indirect kick will be awarded to the opposing team. All of the other throw-in infractions happen before the throw-in has been completed (such as stepping over the line, twisting during the throw, or lifting a foot). In these cases, the throw-in will be awarded to the opposite team.

Notice that rules don't say anything about having to be still during the throw. For that matter, they don't say anything about what happens in the seconds leading up to it. Without getting into physics, let's just say that going into the throw with some momentum is a good thing for getting distance on the ball. For this reason, players will start a few feet off the line and take a short run up to it.

a snapping action at the waist, someone figured out that doing a front flip into the throw-in would generate even more forward momentum and, therefore, enormously increase distance on the ball. Very few players have learned how to do them, and not all leagues allow them, but you'll know one when you see one.

Goal Kicks. When a ball goes outside either goal line, but is not a goal, the referee must decide whether to award a goal kick or a corner kick, based on a recommendation from the assistant referee. If the team attacking the goal on the goal line in question has kicked the ball out, a goal kick will be awarded. To take a goal kick, any player on the defending team may take the ball and place it anywhere within the goal box. Because it is to the defending team's advantage to place the ball as far out from the

Goal Kick Rules

* During a goal kick players from the opposing team must stay outside of the penalty box. If any opposing player enters the box before the ball is in play, the kick will be retaken.

* As with a throw-in, the kicker can't touch the ball again until after another player has touched it. This occurrence is very rare. In fact, the kicker would be hard-pressed to pull this off even if he wanted to. If the kicker does indeed manage to touch the ball again after it has gone into play and before it touches another player, the opposing team will be awarded a free kick from the spot where the second touch occurred. Which type of free kick depends upon how and where he touched it.

* Handball, outside of the box will result in a direct free kick

* Non-handball, outside of the box, will result in an indirect free kick

* Handball, inside of the box, will result in a penalty kick—though I have to say that I can't imagine how the kicker could manage to touch the ball twice within the penalty box before another player does, given that the ball isn't even in play until it has left the penalty box. Oh well, that's what the rule book says.

* Non-handball, inside of the box, will result in a direct free kick

When you think the referee is wrong

Get over it. Seriously. The power of the referee is absolute, and you aren't going to change any- thing by arguing. I sup- pose you could come up with a creative way of questioning the referee's eyesight. (The most cre- ative one I've ever heard, and, I kid you not: "Shake your head ref, your eyes are stuck!") The only thing that you have any hope of accomplishing is causing embarrass- ment for yourself and your child. When it is tempting to get angry, it may be helpful to keep in mind that the referee is watching a lot of very fast-moving action. He will make mistakes. So would you if you were out there. The other thing to keep in mind is that the referee has almost certainly spent more time studying the rulebook than you have. Could there be any chance that the referee is applying a part of the rules you might not understand?

goal line and as far to the side of the goal as possible, this stipulation means that in practice the ball is always placed on one of the two goal box corners.

Corner Kicks. A corner kick happens when a defending player was the last to touch a ball that went over the goal line without being a goal. Defending teams go to great lengths to avoid corner kicks because they can be very dangerous scoring opportunities for the attacking team. Though it isn't common because it is hard to do, the kicker may score di- rectly from the corner kick. The offside rule doesn't apply on corner kicks, so you'll see a mix of attending and defend- ing players jostling around right up to the goal line in the seconds leading up to the kick. To take a corner kick, the kicker must put the ball within the corner circle on the same side of the goal as the ball left the field. She must wait for the ref- eree's signal before taking the kick. And, no, she can't move the annoying little corner flag to take the kick.

While most kickers will do their best to serve the ball up in front of the goal, be sure to watch for close-in kicks too—but these will always be to another player. As with goal kicks, the kicker isn't allowed to touch the ball again until it has touched another player. This means that she can't simply dribble it toward the goal. All other players must stay at least 10 yards from the kicker until the ball is in play. Unlike with goal kicks, the ball need not move far to be considered officially in play. Any movement at all counts.

OFFSIDE

Though perhaps not particularly interesting, most of soccer's laws are at least straightforward and easy to understand. The offside rule has earned a reputation as something fuzzy and difficult to understand. Anecdotally, at least, the offside rule is the most common source of confusion among fans at the game. The good news is that if you break it down to component parts, it really isn't so difficult to understand.

Before a referee will call a player offside, both of the following factors must be present:

1. One or more players must be in an offside position at the time the ball is kicked. (Don't worry—we'll talk about what that means in just a minute).

2. Having been determined to be in an offside position, the offside player(s) also must be an active part of the play.

If both of these factors are indeed present, it is the assistant referee's job to indicate the foul to the referee. This assumes there is an assistant referee, of course, which is not always true. Assuming that one is present, the AR will indicate offside by positioning himself along the touchline in line with the location of the offside player. He will stand with both feet together and the flag raised high overhead. Even if the AR has indicated an offside foul, that doesn't mean that it actually will be called. Remember that in this, as in all things, the referee has the final say. If an AR isn't present for whatever reason, the referee must do the best that he can.

Correctly calling the offside rule is one of the most important functions of the AR. It is often a matter of inches, and it is really hard to see correctly unless the person calling the foul is lined up with the last defender, so as to be in an optimal position to see the foul. That's why you'll see the assistant referees move up and down the field in their respective halves so as to stay in line with the last defender.

Why the last defender? That brings us to our discussion of what exactly constitutes being in an offside position. Even this is relatively simple. To quote the FIFA Laws: A player is in an offside position whenever "he is nearer to his opponents' goal line than both the ball and the second last opponent." Because the goalkeeper almost always is nearer to the goal line than just about anyone, the second to last defender generally translates to the last field-playing defender.

> ### Strange but true facts about being offside
>
> * It is not an offense to simply be in an offside position.
> * There is no such thing as offside on a throw-in, corner kick, or goal kick.
> * A player cannot be offside in his own half.
> * Ties go to the offense. In other words, if the offensive player is level with the defender in question, he will NOT be offside.

HANDBALL

Everyone knows that players can't use their hands in soccer—except of course, for the keeper. So what exactly constitutes a handball and what are the consequences? According to the Laws of the Game, a handball, or a foul for handling, happens whenever a player deliberately touches the ball with the hand or the arm—any touch from the shoulder down is off-limits. That sounds simple enough: it's the deliberate part that brings in the gray area. If a player reaches out and grabs the ball, it is pretty obvious that a handball should be called. But you'll see many referees call a handball even when a player didn't appear to intend to touch the ball at all. In fact, I've seen it called many times when the player wasn't even looking at the ball, let alone reaching for it. You'll usually see this happen if it caused a significant change in the flow of the play. Like so many other fouls, the interpretation of what constitutes a hand ball is completely left to the discretion of the referee.

Whether intentional or not, if a referee calls a foul for handling the ball, the opposing team will be awarded a direct kick. If the player deliberately handles a ball during what the referee considers to be an obvious goal-scoring opportunity, he'll get a red card to boot. What's worse—just about the only opportunity for a player to handle a ball to prevent a goal scoring opportunity occurs within the penalty box, which also means that the opposing team will get a penalty kick out of the situation. With the result being a likely goal and losing a player (for the red card) for the remainder of the game, it is no wonder that you almost never see this happen in play. The penalties are simply too stiff.

AN OVERVIEW OF FREE KICKS

Before we get into describing direct vs. indirect kicks and their associated fouls, there are a few things that apply to ALL free kicks. Penalty kicks are a little different than free kicks, so we'll describe those rules separately.

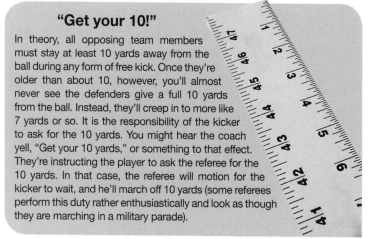

"Get your 10!"

In theory, all opposing team members must stay at least 10 yards away from the ball during any form of free kick. Once they're older than about 10, however, you'll almost never see the defenders give a full 10 yards from the ball. Instead, they'll creep in to more like 7 yards or so. It is the responsibility of the kicker to ask for the 10 yards. You might hear the coach yell, "Get your 10 yards," or something to that effect. They're instructing the player to ask the referee for the 10 yards. In that case, the referee will motion for the kicker to wait, and he'll march off 10 yards (some referees perform this duty rather enthusiastically and look as though they are marching in a military parade).

* The referee will stop play and place the ball at the location of the infraction.

* All defending players must stay at least 10 yards away from the ball.

* The ball must be stationary at the time of the kick.

* The kicker cannot touch the ball again until at least one other player has touched it. In other words, the kicker can't just start dribbling toward the goal.

DIRECT KICKS

A direct free kick is the most basic of the free kicks. The referee stops play, and the ball is placed at the location of the infraction. This type of free kick is called *direct* because the kicker can score directly from the kick. You'll see this type of kick awarded for fouls that are considered serious (or at least relatively so). With that said, it isn't that a referee will decide between a direct or indirect kick on the basis of severity. The type of kick to be awarded is dictated by a specific list of offenses. If the offense is on this list, the referee has no discretion in the type of free kick to award—only whether or not to call the foul at all.

According to the Laws of the Game, a direct kick should be awarded if the referee feels that a player has done any of the following in a manner considered careless, reckless, or using excessive force:

* **Kicking.** Kicking the ball: good. Kicking at another player in the absence of the ball: bad.

* **Tripping.** Intentionally trying to catch the foot of a player passing by is a foul, and one of the easiest for the referee to spot. As players get older, they get more subtle at this one. If you watch closely, you'll see players try to hook their feet around another's in the seconds after a tackle.

* **Jumping.** Jumping straight up, say to head a ball, is fine. It is only

a foul if the referee feels that the player is jumping *into* another player.

* **Charging.** Picture this foul as something akin to a football block. The interpretations section of the Laws of the Game defines this specifically as "challenging for space within playing distance of the ball without using arms or elbows." Remember that for charging to be considered a foul it has to be careless, reckless, or involve excessive force. In the absence of these factors, it is perfectly OK to use a shoulder to lean into another player while trying to win or keep possession of a ball. As long as it doesn't involve elbows or start to look like a football block, there's no problem.

* **Hitting, pushing, or tackling**—or attempts to do any of these things. Enough said.

And these offenses warrant a direct kick even if they are not careless or reckless:

* **Handling the ball intentionally.** (See Handball.)

* **Holding another player.** This one is a little fuzzy. When I was playing, any grabbing of arms, jerseys, hair, etc., was absolutely not

How will I know what kind of kick has been awarded?

Don't feel like memorizing which fouls go with which kind of kick—or harder still, having to figure out exactly what a referee has called? Not to worry, the referee will clearly identify the type of kick that has been awarded with his arm motions.

For a **direct kick**, he will keep one arm horizontal, pointing in the direction that a kick is to be taken (i.e., in the direction of the goal that the kicking team is working toward).

For an **indirect kick**, he will hold one arm straight overhead, lowering it only when a second touch has occurred, meaning that a goal may now be scored.

tolerated. Now, much of it is. Let's just say that my 17-year-old had three jerseys ripped in the last year alone, and I don't think that any of those incidents resulted in fouls.

✱ Spitting at another player. Ick.

INDIRECT KICKS

An indirect kick is a free kick with a catch. All that separates an indirect kick from a direct free kick is that the kicker cannot score directly—that's where the name comes from. At least one other player must touch the ball after the indirect kick before it

WHY ARE ALL THE DEFENDERS LINING UP IN A ROW?

When the opposing team has been awarded a free kick, you should see the defenders scurrying around to get in proper defensive position. If the ball is anywhere within the offensive third of the field, between two and five defenders will rush to form a tight row in front of the kicker and perpendicular to the direction of the kick. This is known as a wall. You'll also see either the keeper or perhaps a forward directing the players to move a little this way or that. The number of players in the wall will depend upon the proximity to the goal. The idea is to block as much of the goal from an easy shot as possible. This is an important defensive strategy. Players ranging from about age 10 all the way to the pros use this strategy.

can be declared a goal. It doesn't matter who touches the ball. It can be another offensive player, a defensive player, or the goalie—anybody but the kicker will do, and any form of touch will be fine.

An indirect free kick will be awarded for offenses that are considered only mildly egregious, such as:

* **Dangerous play.** The most common source of this foul is a kick that comes up above waist level or so for a nearby player. You might hear other fans yelling "Hey! That was a high kick!"

* **Obstruction.** The FIFA Laws call this "impeding the progress of the player," but it is more commonly known as obstruction. The general idea is that a player can't throw his body in front of another player in order to slow him down, *unless* they are both within playing distance of the ball. If they are within playing distance of the ball, it is considered merely shielding the ball, which is quite legitimate and a very useful strategy.

* **Preventing the keeper from releasing the ball.** This one almost never happens because everyone knows you can't stand in front of the keeper all day.

* **Any foul warranting a yellow or red card that is not in the list of fouls subject to a direct kick.** This is sort of a catch-all category.

* **The keeper holds the ball more than six seconds before distributing it to another player.** It used to be that keepers could only take three steps before releasing the ball. Now they've got a full six seconds to get as close to the edge of the penalty box as they can.

* **The keeper picks the ball up again once it has been released and before it has been touched by another player.** This prevents the keeper from getting repeated shots at the six-seconds rule.

* **The keeper picks the ball up with his hands after it has been passed to him or thrown in to him deliberately by a teammate.** This happens all the time, especially among younger keepers who simply forget to pay attention to how the ball came to them in the heat of the moment. If you played growing up, you might remember that passing

the ball back to the keeper was a major tenet of defensive strategy. FIFA decided to disallow this practice a number of years ago because it was leading to low-scoring games. (It had been too effective as a defensive strategy!) You'll still see players pass back to their keepers, but the keepers need to remember not to pick it up. They have to kick it instead. Note that when a defender uses his head to pass the ball back to a keeper, it is not subject to this rule.

Why are there sometimes two kickers?

You might notice that instead of a single kicker lining up for a free kick, there might be two or more. This is done for a couple of reasons. If it is an indirect kick, having multiple kickers allows the option for one player to run across the ball, touching it briefly, which would make it legal for the second kicker to score. If it is a direct kick, the only reason for multiple kickers is to confuse the defense. If you aren't sure who is going to take the shot, it is a little harder to defend.

PENALTY KICKS

The rule for awarding penalty kicks is very simple. One will be awarded if a player commits a foul that would otherwise call for a direct free kick in her team's penalty area (the larger of the two boxes surrounding the goal). Referees do not (and should not) call these fouls lightly, as they can completely change the course of the game. The conversion rate for penalty kicks is extremely high, so when a referee awards one, it is nearly tantamount to awarding a goal.

THE ADVANTAGE RULE

The next time you see a referee hesitate to call a foul, it might look like simple indecision, but probably isn't. American football allows teams to decline penalties to which they would otherwise be entitled. Soccer has a similar provision, except that the referee automatically makes that decision for the team. If the referee sees a foul but feels that the team would benefit more by being allowed

The language of fouls

When you see fouls occurring on the field, you'll probably also hear some special terms thrown around. Here's how to decode them:

* **Cleats up**—A player has gone in to a foul with his cleats exposed. This is only done when trying to foul, and is never necessary when trying to actually get the ball.

* **From behind**—players are not allowed to tackle from behind.

* **Late**—The play may have been OK . . . if only it had taken place during the play rather than after it.

* **No ball** or **all ball**—in order for a tackle to be fair, players must be playing the ball.

to continue playing, he will usually indicate so by holding both arms out horizontally and pointing in the direction of play for the team being given the advantage call. He might also say "play on." If a referee does allow for advantage, he can still call the foul at a later point. Many times, referees will hesitate in order to see if the team can make anything out of the play on their own. If it doesn't pan out, the referee can still stop the play and bring the ball back to the location at which the foul occurred.

YELLOW AND RED CARDS

Some fouls are too severe to go punished only by a simple free kick or penalty kick. In those cases, the referee has another method of punishment at his disposal—yellow and red cards. Those of you with six-year-olds should be spared from seeing these for several years. By the time your player is into the middle school years, they'll be a fairly frequent occurrence. If a player is issued a card, you can say she was "carded" or "booked."

FIFA's Laws of the Game specify a number of specific cautionable offenses, which call for yellow cards and sending-off offenses, which call for red cards. The referee has the authority to issue cards from the time he arrives at the field of play until he leaves the field—even if it is after the final whistle. He also has the authority to issue a card to players who may not even be playing at the time! So what kind of offenses will get a player a card? A yellow card will be given when a referee feels that a player's conduct should be officially cautioned, while a red card will be issued if the offense is serious enough that the player should be sent off the field.

Yellow Cards

Yellow cards get issued fairly frequently. I've not been able to find any specific statistics, but among players middle-school age and up, I'd say that there's probably an average of one yellow card per game or two.

When a yellow card is issued, the referee will record the player's number. This is both to report the card to local officials (some leagues have rules tracking the number of allowable yellow cards in a season), as well to serve as a reminder in case the same player causes trouble later in the game. Depending upon local league rules, the player may have to leave the field for at least one play, but unlike with a red card, another player may be substituted in her place. Whether the player has to leave the field or not, play will be restarted and continued as normal.

Offenses subject to issuance of a yellow card include:

* **General bad behavior** including unsporting behavior, dissent (i.e., yelling at the referee), or persistent fouls (even if the individual offenses are of a less serious nature). This catch-all category means that the referee can issue a card for just about any offense.

* **Delaying any kind of restart in a game,** including a free kick. For example, it isn't acceptable for a player to pick up the ball and hold it to prevent a quick restart from the other team, or to intentionally kick the ball far out of bounds in an obvious attempt to run out the clock.

* **Failing to give the required 10 yards distance** for an opponent's free kick, corner kick, or throw-in. Though the referee is perfectly within his rights to issue a yellow card for this infraction, very few

do. Players are usually smart enough to cheat in to a distance of more like seven yards—close enough in to cause problems for the kicker, but not so close as to draw a card.

* **Entering or leaving the field** without the permission of the referee.

Red Cards

Red cards, on the other hand, are much less common than yellow cards. Because the associated penalties are serious enough that they can impact the outcome of the game, referees tend to be very judicious in their use of red cards. It takes a pretty serious offense to earn one. Even among teams of teenage boys, you might only see a couple of these a season.

When a red card is issued, the player must leave the field immediately and remain out for the remainder of the game. In most cases, the player will also be suspended from the next scheduled game as well, and even multiple games for really serious offenses. Even worse, no substitute may come in to take the ejected player's place. This means, of course, that the team will be a player short for the rest of the game (though they may return to a full squad for the next scheduled game). In a close match, this can be a very significant factor.

Offenses subject to issuance of a red card include serious occurrences of any of the following:

* **Severe fouls of any type.** There is obviously a lot of gray area here, but in the vast majority of cases, you'll recognize a red card-worthy foul when you see it. They tend to be deliberately dangerous.

* **Violence of any kind** (including spitting), foul language, and/or hand gestures.

* **Deliberately using a foul** to stop an *obvious goal-scoring opportunity*. For example, if a defender sees that the ball is about to be a goal and reaches out with his hands in order to prevent the goal, that player will be issued a red card, and ejected from the game.

Advantage/Play On

Yellow/Red Card   Direct Free Kick   Goal Kick

Corner Kick   Throw In   Corner Kick with Flag

Offside   Goal Kick with Flag   Substitution

✳ **Receiving a second yellow card in the same game.** Note that this situation is sometimes called a *soft red* because its consequences are not quite as severe as for a *hard red*. While the player does get ejected from the current game and his team does have to finish the game a man down, there will be no additional suspension.

Why isn't that a foul?!

Referees must consider a whole lot of information when deciding whether or not to call a foul. They have to consider its severity, whether the offended team would benefit from calling the foul, the overall flow of the game, and more. The more cynical soccer fans tend to suggest that referees are biased or supporting the other team. While that does happen sometimes, I really do believe that it is infrequent. If a flagrant foul has not been called, much more often than not, it is because the referee either had a very good reason (perhaps invoking the advantage rule), or he simply didn't see it. As I keep saying, there is a lot for referees to keep track of. Personally, I don't know how they see all of the things they do see.

THE UNWRITTEN RULES OF SOCCER

We've just spent a lot of time talking about the formal rules of soccer. If a player fails to comply with any of those, the referee will be there to remind him, usually with a foul. But there are a few unwritten rules too. There is no official enforcement of these rules, but it is considered bad form to ignore them. Here's how to read between the lines of the rulebook.

HANDS OFF THE KEEPER

A tackle or collision that might be acceptable between two players is not OK when the goalkeeper is involved. Because goalkeepers are exposed and vulnerable, referees tend to be very protective of them, as are the goalkeeper's teammates. It is best for players to show a little bit of extra caution when it comes time to go in for a fifty-fifty ball with a goalkeeper.

DO THE RIGHT THING FOR AN INJURY

When a player goes down with an injury, the referee will look for the first reasonable opportunity to stop play. Sometimes, however, the referee doesn't see the injury, or an opportunity doesn't come quickly enough. In that case, the team with possession of the ball should knock the ball out across the nearest touchline to allow the player to get help. When the play restarts, the rules require that the opposing team be given a throw-in. The team with the throw-in should remember that the only reason they have the ball is because the other team was kind enough to voluntarily stop play. To return the favor, they should throw the ball back to the other team. To do anything else is considered poor sportsmanship.

If, on the other hand, the referee does see the injury and manages to stop play, a drop-ball will be used to restart the play. In theory, a drop ball is supposed to be a fifty-fifty opportunity for either side to win the ball. However, in this case, the team that had been in possession of the ball at the time the play was stopped should be allowed to win the drop-ball without contest. This is such a widely accepted unwritten rule that you may even see the referee simply drop the ball in front of the keeper of the team that should get the ball back.

If the play is stopped for an extended period, you'll often see players of both teams drop down to one knee while the player is attended to. When the injured player either leaves the field or is able to return to play, it is customary for the fans of both teams to clap.

TAKE IT EASY IF YOUR TEAM HAS THE GAME IN HAND

If one team is clearly winning, there is no point in running up the score, and there is no point in going in for aggressive tackles. By the same token, some players find it offensive when the opposing team obviously stops playing altogether. Many coaches will manage this situation by removing their best players from the field, which gives substitutes game experience, but reduces the risk of a completely outbalanced score.

THE GAME ONLY STOPS ON A NEUTRAL PLAY

Even though the game is supposed to be stopped according to time, if you watch closely, you'll rarely, if ever, see a referee stop the game when a team has an imminent scoring opportunity. Instead, the game will usually be called while the ball is in the middle third of the field, often immediately after a defensive clear.

BASIC STRATEGY

While this book is not intended by any means to be a coaching or playing manual, I do think that all spectators stand to enjoy the game more when they have at least a good level understanding of strategy. If nothing else, understanding the concepts here will help you have better postgame conversations with your child.

Before your kids get very far along in their soccer careers, you will hear them bandy about numbers, such as 4-4-2, that make it sound as if they are calling **football plays.** What they are actually referring to is a simple code describing the team's playing formation.

Playing formations are always described using three numbers. The first number gives the number of defenders, the middle number the number of midfielders, and the last number gives the number of forwards. There is no point in specifying the number of goalkeepers of course, because the team has no choice in that matter; they are allowed only one. Obviously, then, the numbers in the formation code must add up to the total number of field players, or ten for teams playing on full-size fields.

For many years, the most common formation has been a 4-4-2, which, to belabor the point, involves four defenders, four midfielders, and two forwards. When there are only two forwards, they must each cover both striker and wing responsibilities. The other common formation is a 4-3-3. It is a more aggressive formation that pushes one of the midfielders up to play forward. While you may occasionally hear of formations including five players in a single position, they are not at all common.

TEAM COMPOSITION

In any good recipe or a musical composition, the quality of the final product depends upon making the best use of the individual elements available to you, whether they are ingredients or instruments. The same is true for soccer teams. When a coach is deciding where to position a particular player,

Don't pass it backwards! That's the wrong way!

Actually, good soccer strategy calls for players to use all of their teammates, whether they happen to be in front, behind, or next to them. Listen for phrases like "You've got drop!" or "Support," which are on-field communication phrases used to indicate that a player has the option of passing behind him. Sometimes dropping the ball briefly back allows for the team to avoid a congested area, perhaps switching the ball to an entirely new area with lots of open space.

she must consider not only the player's individual strengths and personality, but also the strengths and personalities of the remaining team members, as well as the team's playing strategy. For example, if a coach has six players who normally play midfield, but only two forwards, she will have to convert some of those midfielders to at least back-up forwards. In another example, a coach may find that a player who played well at defense on past teams is better suited to midfield with the formation and strategy used by the current coach. Any way you look at it, placing players into positions is a delicate balancing act. If your child's coach moves your child into a new position, try not to prejudge. Have some faith that the coach has thought it through for the benefit of the team as a whole.

ON-FIELD COMMUNICATION

A team that can't work together won't do very well and, worse, won't have any fun. And the only way to work together, of course, is to communicate. The tricky part is that players have only seconds (if that) to decide what to do with the ball next, so any communication has got to be concise and unambiguous. Over time a soccer shorthand of sorts has developed that is shockingly consistent from field to field and team to team.

HERE'S WHAT THEY REALLY MEAN WHEN THEY SAY . . .

* "Man-on." An opposing player is coming at you quickly, probably from a direction that you can't see, so you'd better think about get-

WHEN SHOULD PLAYERS SPECIALIZE IN A GIVEN POSITION?

Although there has been a trend toward earlier position specialization, most experts recommend against this. You should try to encourage your player (and your player's coach!) to experiment with all of the positions until the early teen years. Playing all of the positions at a young age has a couple of advantages. First, it gives a player a chance to learn what each position is all about so that she can determine the best match for her own strengths and characteristics. Second, spending time at each position enables a player to become more well-rounded and, therefore, a much better player down the road. For example, forwards are regularly called upon to defend in one-on-one situations. Having spent time in defensive positions, she'll have had an opportunity to learn the position's finer points. Likewise, a defender who has had the chance to play forward will have a better understanding for how a forward thinks and will, therefore, be better positioned to anticipate an opposing player's moves. Players will start to gravitate to one or two positions by the teenage years. If they've already gained a breadth of knowledge by playing all positions earlier in their careers, they will be ready to gain the deep intuition that comes with developing a specialty in a position.

ting rid of that ball. And fast.

* "You've got drop," or simply "drop." I'm right behind you and am open to receive a pass.

* "Square." I'm directly next to you and am available to receive a pass.

* "Switch." It has become way too crowded on this side of the field, so I think you should make a long pass to the other side of the field.

* "Overlap." I'm going to hold on to the ball for a minute. I want you to continue running past me and I'll pass you the ball.

* "Carry." Keep dribbling.

* "Hold." Hang onto the ball just a minute—help is on the way.

* "Yeah" or "Yes." Pass to me, I'm open. (You might also just hear the open player call the name of the player with the ball to get her attention.)

* "Through" or "Play me through." I'm going to run behind a defender. I want you to pass the ball so that when I come open on the other side of the defender I can run onto the ball.

* "Cross." Pass the ball to a player across the field from you.

* "Have it." Take a shot.

* "Mine," "My ball," or "I go." I'll try to win this fifty-fifty (uncontrolled) ball. Don't crash into me, please.

* "I got 4" (or 6 or 13 or 11 for that matter). I'm marking number 4 from the opposing team, so you should go worry about somebody else.

A FEW PHRASES YOU MIGHT HEAR DEFENDERS SAYING TO EACH OTHER:

* "You've got support" I'm here behind you, so if you want to go ahead and try to win the ball from the offensive player, I can back you up.

* "Go to ball." Go ahead and try to win the ball (as opposed to hanging back to mark another player).

* "Clear." Things are looking pretty desperate. Just kick the ball as far up the field as you can manage, even if you can't get it to anyone specific.

* "No shot." I don't care what else you do or where else you let him pass, just don't let him take a shot.

* "No foul." I know you're tempted to knock that player over, but we really can't afford to get (a) another card or (b) give up a penalty kick, so please remember to keep your cool.

THERE ARE A FEW STANDARD NON-VERBAL SIGNALS TOO.

* A player without the ball might hold an arm up directly overhead to indicate he is ready and willing to receive a pass. Alternatively, he may hold both arms in front of him with palms out and pointing toward his feet.

* A player about to take a free kick will often raise an arm overhead to indicate that he's about to take the kick.

* A player wishing to receive a through pass will start running while holding one arm out horizontally and pointing in the direction he'd like the pass to be made.

THE PLAYING FIELD

You will often hear me refer to the playing field or the pitch, as if they are all the same. They aren't. The size and type of surface of the playing field will vary dramatically among different ages, different parts of the country, and even different fields within the same public park.

FIFA rules require that a regulation field (i.e., one used by professional teams or others in a FIFA-sanctioned match) be:

* Rectangular in shape

* Longer along the touchline (sideline) than along the goal line

* Between 100 and 130 yards in length and 50 to 100 yards wide

Any field size within those parameters is, as they say, fair game. Even among the professional teams, there is no field size standardization. In the British Premier League, for example, you will find home pitches ranging in size from Manchester City's enormous field at City of Manchester Stadium (116 x 77 yards) to the relatively tiny Boleyn Ground, home to West Ham United (110 x 70 yards). In the USA's Major League Soccer organization, the Colorado Rapids play on a field that is 120 x 80 yards, while DC United's field is only 110 x 70 yards.

If even the professionals can't expect to find standard field sizes, it stands to reason that your kids won't either. In fact, field sizes must conform to the available area of the complex or stadium containing the field. In some cases, it has been reported, managers will request that a field's dimension be changed to better accommodate their team's particular style of play.

Where young players are concerned, I suppose you also can say that field sizes are changed to accommodate style of play. The younger and lower skilled the players, the smaller the field size should be. While field sizes are all over the map, there are some general guidelines that you can expect.

PROGRESSION FROM MICRO TO FULL-SIZE

The very smallest players—called micro players in many areas—also use the very smallest fields and the smallest goals. Using smaller fields for smaller players was a long time in coming and was a welcome development. When little players play on very large fields, they simply don't have as much fun. By keeping the fields and goals to an age-appropriate size, players get to experience more touches on the ball and more chances on goal—both of which are very motivating. This set-up also makes it possible to teach and reinforce fundamental concepts of team play such as support and quick passes. If players have to resort to long kicks up the field, or if they spend all of their time running back and forth, they will lose much of the enjoyment of the game. If your recreational league is using full-size fields for small players, please, for your child's sake, lobby for reduced field sizes.

Like many local leagues, our local community soccer commission has specified field sizes that grow progressively by age group. The youngest players in the under-6 (U6) age group play on a 30- x 20-yard field with proportionately small 4- x 6-foot goals. The U7 age group steps up just a bit to 40 x 25 yards, but continues to use the 4- x 6-foot goals. At the U8 to U9 level there is a large bump-up in both field and goal size; the field is 70 x 40 yards, while the goal is 5 x 15 feet. The U10-U12 age groups play on a field that is closer still to full size at 95 x 55 yards with 6.5- x 18-foot goals. Finally, at ages U13 and up, the fields reach a full size of 110 x 65 yards, with the standard 8-foot x 8-yard goals. There is every chance that your child's fields won't match these sizes exactly, but these should at least give you a general idea of what to expect.

What are all of those Field Markings?

All but the very smallest of fields contain standardized markings. So what do they all mean, and how do they impact play?

① Goal line

The two goal lines lie along the shorter dimension of the outer rectangle of a soccer field. As the name implies, the goal lines represent the target for players. The goal will rest along the goal line. Any ball that is between the goal posts and crosses the line completely is a goal.

② Touchline/Sideline

Either of the two long sides of the field rectangle. You will frequently hear these called the sidelines. Either term is fine, and everyone will understand what you mean, but hardcore soccer

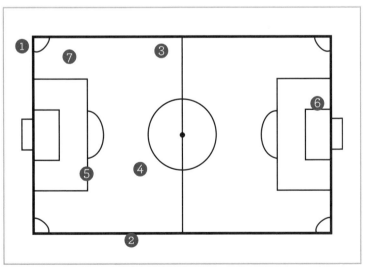

purists prefer the term touchline.

③ MIDFIELD LINE

This line denotes, exactly as you would expect, the halfway point between the two opposing goals. Players will line up along this line for every kickoff. The other time that it becomes significant is in relation to the offside rule; a player cannot be offside if he is on the same side of the midfield line as the goal that his team is defending.

④ CENTER CIRCLE

Located in the center of the field, and 10 yards in diameter, this center circle comes into play only during kickoffs. When the two opposing teams line up for kick-off, the team with the kick-off will place the ball at the very center of the circle. The opposing team must remain on its own side of the midfield line, and outside of the center circle.

⑤ PENALTY BOX

The penalty box, commonly abbreviated as the box, is arguably the most important marking on the field, other than perhaps the field perimeter. Measuring 18 x 44 yards on a regulation field, the penalty box impacts play in two ways. First, the goalkeeper can use her hands only within the confines of the penalty box. One direct result of this rule is that a goalkeeper must punt the ball from within the penalty box. Second, fouls that are committed within the penalty box may result in a penalty kick. Penalty kicks are a big deal; such a big deal in fact, that they often change the outcome of the game. Penalty kicks are taken from a spot marked 12 yards out from the midpoint of the goal posts. While a penalty kick is being taken, only the keeper and shot-taker are allowed within the penalty area. All other players must stay outside of the box and outside of a circle with a radius of 10 yards centered on the penalty spot. Most fields are marked with the portion of the circle that falls outside the penalty area. When watching a game on a full-size field, you might hear someone refer to taking a shot from the 18. That's because the outermost edge of the penalty box on a regulation field is 18 yards from the goal line. The dimensions of the penalty box will be proportionately smaller on a smaller field and may be absent altogether on a micro field.

❻ GOAL BOX

This box, measuring 6 x 20 yards on a regulation field, is located directly in front of each goal. The ball must be placed within the goal box for goal kicks. Because goal kicks usually are kicked along one side of the field or the other, and because it is to the advantage of the team taking the goal kick to place the ball as far into the field as possible, this restriction means that in practice, the ball is always placed on one of the two corners of the goal box.

❼ CORNER CIRCLES

Most fields are marked with quarter circles with a one-yard radius in each of the field's four corners. The ball must be placed within the corner circle for any corner kick.

4 Tournaments: Taking It on the Road

If your career as a Soccer Mom lasts more than a couple of years, you almost certainly will participate in a soccer tournament or two per year per child. What exactly is a tournament? The answer to that question depends in part upon who you ask. There are tournaments and then there are Tournaments with a capital T. For our purposes, we'll define a tournament as any organized soccer-playing experience consisting of two or more games within a short span of time.

According to our definition, then, a tournament could include anything from an informal pre-season jamboree for young recreational players to a national and fiercely competitive gathering of elite-level players. In this section, we'll review what to expect during tournaments and provide mom-tested tips for surviving them gracefully.

WHAT TO EXPECT

Most tournaments take place in the summer. They range from local, casual tournaments that include recreational divisions to elite, national-level tournaments. A few of the most renowned elite youth tournaments are by invitation only, and are almost as hard to get into than a Manchester United vs. Arsenal match.

Most tournaments are divided by age group. Within each age group, there may be multiple divisions ranked by competitive level. Finally, all of the teams within a single division may be separated into pools, depending upon how many teams have entered. Placement in pools is usually random, but in some tournaments, there may be some seeding going on. This just means that the most competitive teams are deliberately placed into separate pools so that there is less chance that they will eliminate each other in the early rounds.

Within pools, it is common that teams will play a preliminary round-robin. In other words, each team in the pool will play each other team. At the end of the round-robin, the team with the most points advances to the next round. In the preliminary rounds, ties generally are allowed to stand.

Teams advancing from the preliminary rounds are matched in elimination rounds, so called because teams losing their games during these rounds are eliminated from the tournament. Elimination rounds, for obvious reasons, are not allowed to stand in a tie. If a tournament is very large, there may be quarterfinal, semifinal and final matches. Smaller tournaments usually will have a preliminary round followed by semifinals and finals.

How Do Tournaments Differ from League Games?

Actually, tournament games don't differ all that much from league games. Each tournament will have its own rules. Tournament game lengths, for example tend to be a bit shorter than standard league games. If a regular league game uses 40-minute halves, tournament games for the same age group might only be 30-minute halves. Tournaments do this to save the legs of players who may have to play multiple games in a single day, and also to help squeeze more games into the schedule. Remember that there will be multiple divisions for each of many age groups.

Tournament-specific rules also will dictate whether games are allowed to stand at a tie. Most regular leagues will allow games to end in a tie. In a tournament, round-robin-style preliminary games may be allowed to stand in a tie, but later round games will not. Obviously then, the tournament directors need a definite conclusion. Tournament rules will specify exactly how this decision will be reached. You can take a deep sigh of relief that tournaments don't use the play-three-years-if-you-have-to-until-somebody-scores method of hockey—at least no tournament I've ever heard of.

Again, every tournament is different, but a common procedure is to play two short overtime periods, usually 10-15 minutes each in length. In some tournaments, the overtime periods include a golden goal provision. Also known as sudden death overtime, this provision means that the first team to score wins. A standard overtime will be played to its full length, even if a team has scored. Teams switch sides at the conclusion of the first overtime period and restart the second period by means of a kick-off.

If the score remains tied after the conclusion of both overtime periods, the game will be decided by the dreaded penalty kicks. Some tournaments, in the interest of time, will skip the overtime periods altogether and go straight to penalty kicks. Trust me when I say that losing a game by penalty kicks is no fun. For that matter, once the initial excitement dies down, it isn't that fun to win a game

How are points calculated?

So how are points given? The precise rules vary widely from tournament to tournament. Here's a typical example:

* 3 points for a win
* 1 point for a tie
* 0 points for a loss
* 1 additional point for a shut out (winning without allowing the other team to score)
* 1 point per goal scored, up to a threshold like 3

In this example, a team who played three games in a preliminary round, winning the first game 3-0, tying the second 1-1 and losing the last 1-2, will be awarded:

* 3 (win) + 1 (shut-out) + 3 (goals) = 7 points for the first game
* 1 (tie) + 1 (goal) = 2 points for the second game
* 0 (loss) + 1 (goal) = 1 point for the third game
* For a grand total of 7+2+1= 10 points for the round

that way either. Still, unless we want games to go on indefinitely, there has to be some final way of deciding them.

COMMUNITY TOURNAMENTS

Your child's first soccer tournament experiences probably will start in your community. In fact, she may play a tournament before she ever plays in her first league game. That's because many U6 leagues now start with pre-season jamborees in which young players are introduced to the fun of the game by getting to play several short, small-sided games in a single afternoon.

Tournaments usually run over a long weekend. Some will start on Friday afternoons, with the finals on Sunday, while others will start on Saturday with finals on Monday morning. For this reason, Memorial Day and Labor Day weekends are very popular choices for tournament directors. You might as well resign yourself now to the fact that these weekends will be occupied by soccer in the years to come.

TOURNAMENT SURVIVAL GUIDE

Though the level of play can vary dramatically between tournaments, the survival skills needed as a mom are more related to the travel distance than the quality of the competition your child will face upon arrival.

Be prepared. Depending upon the format of the tournament and how close the field is to your home, you may or may not be able to return home between games. Be prepared to take extra food and water along. The kids will want some means to occupy themselves in between games. As much as I hate to say it, hand-held video games often work well because they are easy to toss in a bag, and let the kids rest physically. Of course, I would prefer they read a good book, but we don't always get what we want.

Remember that you will be outside—a lot. Be prepared for any kind of weather. If the tournament is in the summer, be sure you have extra sunscreen and a way to keep everyone cool. For tournaments that take place outside of the summer months, be prepared to deal with rain and mud. Even if you have sunny, dry weather, the wind could be blowing. Think extra clothes, and warm gear. One of my Soccer Mom friends in Colorado finds herself reaching for the ski gear for spring tournaments.

Either way, this is a good time to review the recommendations in the Equipment Section. Because you can't just pop home if something was forgotten, you have to plan a little more carefully. Be sure that you've got extra aspirin, extra socks, extra shinguards . . . well, extra most anything.

For yourself, bring the same items that you use to keep yourself occupied during practices or soccer's other wait times. Tournaments can be a great social opportunity, too. Why not take the chance to get better acquainted with your fellow parents?

Though many tournaments now offer food vendors, you can't always count on this feature. Better to be prepared with healthy snacks and drinks from home. This is especially true if your games will span normal meal times.

M⚽m Tip

Don't be in a hurry

Tournaments often run late, so don't take their timelines too much at face value. Make arrangements as necessary so that the world won't come to an end if you have to stay a little longer. After all, your team may very well win the whole thing. You wouldn't want to have to run off before the medal ceremony, would you?

TRAVELING WITH THE TEAM

This section could be subtitled *How to Feed 15 Starving and Smelly 16 Year Olds with Grace and Aplomb*. A travel, or away, tournament is any tournament that takes place far enough from home that it requires an overnight stay.

This probably will mean that you will be driving around in an unfamiliar city looking for fields, so a GPS would come in awfully handy. Failing that, bring maps. And don't forget a cell phone list, so that you can call the other parents to set you on the right track after you've taken a wrong turn.

Choosing a Team Hotel

It is a lot of fun for the kids—and parents, too—to stay in the same hotel. It makes logistics a lot easier (a handful of parents can drive the kids over to their warm-up, allowing the majority of the parents to come later at game time), and it makes post game time activities a lot more fun.

When choosing a hotel, here are a few things to look for:

* A pool

* An included buffet breakfast

* Reasonable proximity to the fields

* Early check-out without penalties. You may be eliminated earlier than you think. If your player can't go home with a tournament medal, it would at least be nice consolation to go home with a little more money in your pocket.

* Late check-out for at least a handful of rooms. It is common to have two games on the last day of the tournament: semifinals in the morning and finals in the evening. It is nice to have a place to leave extra luggage and gear and to allow for between-game showers if necessary.

* In-room kitchenettes, to prepare lunches or meals

* Public barbecues, for cooking dinner main dishes

* In-room refrigerators, for storing snacks and keeping drinks cool

* Free internet. Not only will the kids want to check their Facebook pages, but it also is helpful for finding restaurants, local activities, field directions, and checking the weather.

* On-site laundry facilities, or at least a nearby Laundromat, just in case you deal with mud or will be on the road for several games.

Feeding the Kids

Team dinners in a local restaurant can be fun on occasion, but it wears pretty thin if you go to many travel tournaments. For one thing, you'll have to wait for an eternity for a group that large to be seated. OK, maybe not that long, but it feels like it after a long day on the field. It also takes extra time for the kitchen to coordinate the meals for such a large group, and it takes forever to sort out the bill. If you still are mid-tournament, the kids are tired and starving. Despite its disadvantages, this is what most teams still do.

Fortunately, I have seen a better way. My son played for a while with a very elite team that was used to traveling nationwide for tournaments. There was a core group of parents who traveled with them. Watching them in action was a thing of beauty. It was obvious that they'd done this many times and had it down to a science. The boys were well fed and well taken care of. But better yet, this feat was accomplished more efficiently and at a far lower cost than the standard eat-every-meal-out approach. It even left them enough time to work on homework, which made the moms among the group happy!

This is their basic procedure:

Each player's family contributes a pre-set amount for food up front, collected prior to the tournament. Immediately upon arrival, a couple of volunteers take the team funds to Costco or equivalent to buy:

* Sandwich fixings: buns, lunch meats, lettuce, tomatoes, condiments, peanut butter, jelly, etc.

* Fruit: apples, bananas, grapes, etc.

* Drinks (waters, juices, electrolyte drinks)

* Carbohydrate-based side dish ingredients (pasta, rice, potatoes)

* Chicken, hamburger, etc.

* Burger fixings

* Salad ingredients

* Paper plates, forks, napkins, etc.

* Healthy snacks: whole grain bagels, nuts, etc.

Breakfast is eaten at the hotel's included buffet breakfast (You chose a hotel with an included breakfast, right?)

For each lunch, a couple of parents commandeer the hotel's breakfast area (with the permission of the management of course), pull a few tables together, and lay out sandwich fixings and fruit. Players come along in buffet fashion and make their own sandwiches.

For dinner, volunteers cook dinner's main dish on the hotel's public barbecues, while other volunteers use their in-room kitchenette to make large pans of rice or spaghetti. Set out the side dishes along with main dish, fruit, and salad again in the breakfast area, again in buffet style.

Any time that the team is back at the hotel between games, healthy snacks like fruit, bagels and nuts can be placed out for the kids to take as desired. And believe me, they'll take. Unless you've already seen it for yourself, you can't imagine the quantity of food that a group of 15 teenagers can consume in a short period of time.

While this sounds like more work and more time consuming for the parents, it isn't. In fact, even including prep time and clean-up, it is much faster and cheaper than eating in restaurants. Plus, you can have more control over what the kids eat, and be sure they get healthy food and plenty of it. It takes a bit more preplanning, but I've seen it work like a dream.

IDEAS FOR BETWEEN GAMES

If you can, take the opportunity to get players out of the elements. While it is nice for them to cheer on friends who may be playing on other teams (especially during the teenage years), getting them out of the sun (or cold as the case may be) is important. If you aren't taking the self-catering approach described in *Feeding the Kids*, then taking them to get lunch in an air-conditioned deli is always a good idea. Just remember to consult the section on *Sports Nutrition and Hydration* for suitably healthy suggestions.

If you have an extended period between games that doesn't fall at a meal time, I can't think of a better activity than taking them to a movie. The very nature of the activity gets them to sit still, relax, and be out of the elements. Many kids like to return to the hotel and take a swim. That's OK as long as it is treated as a chance to cool off, rather than play time or sunbathing time. Many moms like to stake out nearby shopping malls. I can't imagine anything less interesting, but I hear that I'm unusual in this regard. I don't think it is a great idea for players to go shopping between games, because they will need all the rest they can get.

Once all of the games are over, you have many more activity options. I've heard that one team likes to play laser tag after games, for example, and swims in the hotel pool are always popular—especially among teenagers if teams of the opposite gender are around!

5 Equipment

Like any other passion or hobby, getting the most out of the soccer experience requires a few accessories—not just for players, but for parents as well. We briefly covered the bare essentials that are more than enough to get your child started, but you'll soon find that (1) she'll be very quickly asking for more (it's cool stuff, and so-and-so from the team has it) and (2) you may wish you had a few of the items that make Soccer-Momming a little more convenient or pleasant.

The trouble is that there is a bewildering array of soccer-related equipment and accessories out there—some of it worthwhile, some of it not so much. Did you know that there are five different major types of cleats? And that's just the shoes! To help you navigate through the sporting goods store confidently and frugally, here's the essential guide to what your soccer family may need.

FOR YOUR CHILD

Soccer doesn't require much equipment relative to other sports. But there are a few tools of the trade that will help your child play more comfortably. Some pieces of equipment are required and some are merely optional.

If you haven't checked out a soccer specialty store or catalog lately, prepare to be overwhelmed by the bewildering array of equipment, accessories, clothing, training aids and more.** The players think it is all great and that they must have the latest and greatest equipment. But then, they aren't usually footing the bill. Here's the mom-to-mom straight talk about what all of the player equipment is for, what's truly necessary, what's handy, and what's just a waste of money. That way you'll be prepared to negotiate the next time your player tries to insist that he simply must have XYZ.

Your First Trip to the Sporting Goods Store

The good news is that if you have a young, first-time player, your first equipment-buying trip doesn't have to be too painful. There are only a few truly essential items. Since your child is likely to outgrow anything before he could possibly wear it out, quality isn't a big concern. And it isn't like he has to worry about being able to get a fine feel for the ball—he's not going to have any decent feel for it anyway, no matter how much you spend. Simply head to the closest sporting goods store or soccer specialty shop and ask for these essentials by name:

* Cleats
* Shinguards
* Soccer socks

The lowest cost version of any of these items would be just fine. If you want to get detailed buying advice for these items, by all means read ahead. But if this is your child's first taste of the sport, you really don't need read any further at this point. Just know that the information will still be here and ready for you when you need it. And you will if your child continues to play more than a few seasons.

CLEATS

Known as boots to the crowd who refer to soccer as football, this is literally where the rubber meets the road, or more accurately, where the injection-molded plastic meets the grass. Cleats are arguably the most important piece of equipment you will need to buy for your player. And, yes, they are most definitely needed for outdoor soccer. Period. If you don't believe me, try playing a little backyard pick-up game with your kids in regular street shoes. Unless you happen to be playing on a very hard surface with very short, dry grass, you will find yourself slipping and sliding around. You also will find it difficult to feel the ball, or to control its movement. A proper pair of cleats helps to prevent injury, aids in the agility necessary to play, and improves a player's feel for the ball.

Pass on the hand-me-downs

While I'm all for thrift and reuse in general, this is one area where you might want to think twice about using hand-me-downs. If at all possible, it is best to buy new cleats for your player. Each person's foot shape and stride create custom patterns of wear over time. If these cleats are then given to another child, they may be at odds with the new recipient's biomechanics, and could potentially lead to injury.

How Much to Budget

Though having a good-quality, properly fitting pair of cleats is extremely important, that doesn't mean that you have to go all out and buy the most expensive pair on the market. Depending on whether you are still buying from the youth or adult sections, you could easily pay upwards of $200 per pair if buying the best. This truly isn't necessary until a player reaches a very high skill level. It is my firm belief that most youth players do not have sufficient skill to even notice the finely nuanced differences between a moderate pair of cleats and an expensive one. That doesn't mean that your player won't beg and plead for the model worn by their favorite professional player.

The M⚽m Bargain

My policy always has been to contribute the dollar amount necessary to buy what I deemed to be a *reasonable* pair of cleats for the current age and skill level. If my sons wanted anything more elaborate (read: expensive), they were free to contribute the extra dollars required themselves.

Expect to pay around $30 for a decent starter pair of cleats for a very young player. By the time your player is 13 or 14, you'll likely be dealing with adult sizes and, therefore, adult prices. Good quality cleats in adult sizes will be in the neighborhood of $100-$150. As we'll see in just a moment, you may need to buy multiple pairs, as well.

Choosing the Right Type

Having decided on an approximate budget, I'm afraid that your cleat-buying decisions are far from over. Cleats come in several different types, each designed for a specific category of field surface:

* **Firm ground:** By far the most versatile of the five major types, firm ground cleats are designed for firm natural surfaces. They are appro-

priate for use on almost all natural grass and artificial FieldTurf®-type surfaces. These surfaces are characterized by a moderate amount of give, allowing cleat studs to sink slightly into the ground during play, which in turn generates traction. Firm ground cleats feature a medium number of short molded studs. The exact shape of the studs and their pattern on the outsole varies by manufacturer and model. Because of their versatility, firm ground cleats are the most popular type used. Virtually all players should have a pair of firm ground cleats in their gear bags.

* **Soft ground:** As the name suggests, these cleats are designed specifically for softer conditions, as typically occur in areas where conditions are rainy and muddy. On soft fields, studs have a tendency to sink in deeply. If the studs are too close together or too short, mud becomes trapped between them and renders them useless for traction. To counteract this problem, soft ground cleats feature fewer, but longer studs. Traditionally, the studs on soft ground cleats were replaceable, but there seems to be a trend now toward non-removable bladed studs. In fact, some leagues have banned the use of removable studs for safety reasons, so check your league regulations before you buy this type. Having played my college career in Washington state, I can say unequivocally that these make an enormous difference on a soggy, muddy natural field. On the flip side, these are NOT appropriate for general use. If soft ground cleats are worn

on an overly firm surface that does not allow the studs to sink in deeply, the studs will create pressure points that can be painful and often result in bruising. The need for soft ground cleats may diminish over time as the new artificial FieldTurf® surfaces become more prevalent.

* **Hard ground:** Some areas have a tad less rainfall than say, the Pacific Northwest, where I live, and as a result have very hard, sunbaked field surfaces. If you happen to live in or have a child who plays regularly in one of these areas (such as southern California (where I grew up), Colorado, or Texas), you may want to consider a pair of hard ground cleats. These cleats have even more studs than do firm ground cleats. The studs are also shorter and more evenly spaced. The design of hard ground cleats assumes that they are going to sink very little, if at all, into the soil. They also work well on frozen ground.

* **Turf:** This type of cleat came to prevalence during the heyday of old-style artificial turf. They do not use studs, but rather have a sort of serrated/bladed bottom that allows for good traction without creating pressure points from studs that can't sink into the ground. While the very hard style of artificial turf is becoming rarer, this style of cleat is still useful for training and for indoor play.

* **Indoor:** When indoor soccer was just getting started, players would generally use turf shoes. Today, there are custom-designed shoes for indoor play. They usually have non-marking soles and no studs. As the length of the soccer season continues to expand, we are seeing more and more indoor training sessions during the winter months. For this reason, it is useful to have a pair of indoor shoes on hand. Besides, they double as great street shoes.

Ultimately, the type of cleat you choose should come down to the type of field your child will play on most often. In most cases, all of the fields in your area will be of the same type, which will allow your child to get by with a single pair of cleats. Older kids who are traveling over great distances may encounter widely varying field conditions and, therefore, may find it worthwhile to carry two or more pairs of cleats. Most of the members of my southern California-based travel team, for example, owned two pairs of cleats, one each of firm ground and turf. When I went to play college soccer in Washington state, I quickly learned that I'd need to add a soft ground pair as well. My boys, who have grown up playing primarily in Washington, each managed fine with a single pair of firm ground cleats for outdoor and a pair of indoor shoes for the indoor training sessions and use as street shoes. Once they started playing on travel teams, however, field conditions started to vary enough that they began to ask for soft ground cleats. If budget constraints require you to stick to only one pair of cleats, I'd recommend that you buy a pair designed for firm ground. You can get by with firm ground cleats on a soft surface, but not the other way around.

MATERIALS AND CONSTRUCTION

In the old days, quality cleats always meant leather uppers. While you will still find high-end cleats with natural leather uppers, you also will find very high-end cleats with high-tech synthetic uppers. Look for an upper that feels comfortable to your player. A good upper will be thin and flexible to allow for a good feel for the soccer ball. Among natural leathers, kangaroo leather is a favorite because it provides those qualities, but it also comes at a price. In all but teenage players, durability is not as much of an issue as a comfortable fit because, in my experience, the cleats will be outgrown long before they are worn out.

Other considerations include the type of sole used and lacing system. Higher-end cleats now often sport outsoles made of special composite materials, including carbon fiber. I'm not necessarily convinced that these make much of a difference for youth soccer, but they do have the advantage of being light yet strong. One recent innovation that does seem to be catching on is an off-set lacing system. It is one of those simple ideas that makes sense. By moving the laces away from the instep, they no longer interfere with the primary striking area of the foot. As with so many of the equipment features, this is only likely to be significant for older, more advanced players.

PROPER FIT

Unlike with uniforms, you should *not* buy cleats with room to grow. In order for your child to get a proper feel for the ball, it is very important that the cleats fit properly—and a proper fit is a bit snug if anything. When it comes time to go shopping, make sure you have your child wear proper soccer socks so that you can check the true fit. The toe should not be right up against the end, but should be close. You should check that there is less than a thumb-width between the end of the shoe and your child's toe when he is standing up. It is not uncommon for players to wear half a size smaller in cleats than they would in their street shoes. The fit should be snug in the heel and toe, but the width should be comfortable.

Care of cleats

Cleats are going to get wet eventually, and they will most certainly get muddy—unless of course they are used solely indoors. Still, moisture is the enemy. Your player's cleats will last longest if they are wiped down regularly and allowed to dry out between wearing, a goal that is not always possible, but a goal nonetheless. If cleats become very wet during a game or training session, have your player wipe them down with a damp cloth and stuff them with newspaper. If you've chosen a pair made of natural leather, consider treating them with a commercially available preparation to prevent water absorption. Many of the mid- to high-range cleats now come with a breathable cloth storage bag, which is much preferable to a plastic bag that would keep in moisture.

UNIFORM

A soccer uniform, also called a strip or a kit is a color-coordinated set made up of a jersey, shorts, and socks. Some teams also will add mandatory accessory items, such as a warm-up suit, rain jacket, equipment bag, and training jersey. In addition, most elite-level teams require two full strips, one each in a light and dark color. In all likelihood, you will have little or no choice about the uniform your child will wear. Uniform specifications usually are laid out by the league. For that reason, I won't spend any time explaining what to look for in a uniform and will focus instead on what you can expect.

The cost for acquiring a uniform will vary tremendously depending upon both the age of the player and the level of play. If you have a very young player in a recreational league, you may not have to buy a special uniform at all. As kids are getting started, the official uniform often consists of a colored T-shirt that may or may not have a silk-screened number on the back. Players are asked to wear the shorts and socks of their choice. Many recreational leagues purchase uniforms for reuse year after year. In this situation, a uniform is assigned to a player at the beginning of the year and will be returned to the league at the end of the year. The cost for the use of a recreational league uniform is included in league registration fees.

The quality of the uniform chosen by a team tends to increase proportionately as the level of play increases (or as they start to take themselves more seriously!). The jerseys for select and elite teams ages 12 and up usually are made out of technical fabric that has been designed to wick moisture and manage heat transfer. You also should expect—and this is a more significant expectation than the type of fabric—that the cost of this uniform will *not* be included in league fees. The good news is that you probably can use the uniform for two to three years, unless the child changes teams, the team changes equipment vendors, or you neglected to order a size that accommodates a couple of years of growth. Because it is common for siblings to follow in each other's footsteps, it also is possible that you can hand one child's uniform down to another.

Jersey

Jerseys are typically the most expensive part of the basic uniform. The nicer jerseys worn by older kids in non-recreational leagues will run in the neighborhood of $40-$75 each, and you probably will be asked to buy two of them. If your child is playing in a local recreational league, you likely will be asked to buy only one jersey, if any at all, and it probably will be more in the $25-$40 range. Once kids get above the age of 15 of so, they are much harder on jer-

Buy it big

When it comes time to buy your player's uniform, consider ordering a size that is a touch big—at least for the jersey. That way, you'll have some hope of getting an extra year or two's worth of wear out of it. Fortunately, the fact that most players enjoy having a looser fit in their jersey allows us parents to get away with this money-stretching tactic.

seys. This is especially true of boys. My 17-year-old son has had three jerseys ripped in the normal course of play in the past year.

Shorts

You will be happy to hear that shorts tend to be much less expensive and are more likely to be usable for several years. As with the jerseys, the higher-end the team your child plays for, the higher-end the shorts that are required. Nice shorts tend to cost around $40, but can easily be in excess of $50. If you are allowed to choose your own shorts, there are plenty of reasonable options available for under $20. That's good news, because your player will need to have several pairs for use in training.

Socks

The last part of the main uniform is a pair of socks. They are the least expensive, at roughly $10-$20 per pair. Game socks will be at the higher end of that range, while training socks will be at the lower end. It is an obvious point, but I'll make it anyway—socks get grungy quickly. Expect to go through two to four pairs (or so) per season.

Emergency socks

I can't even count all of the pairs we have around our house now, and that doesn't even mention all of the mismatched ones. Because it is so easy for individual socks to go astray, it has been an all too common occurrence to arrive at a field missing a sock. For this reason, I highly recommend keeping an emergency pair in the car for just such an occasion.

Base Layers

Undershirts made of technical fabrics are popular for cool weather play, particularly among older players. Specifically designed to be worn underneath uniforms or a loose training shirt, these shirts are very stretchy and have a compression, second-skin fit so that they do not interfere with a player's comfort or noticeably change the fit of the uniform. They are available for $20-$50 in both short- and long-sleeve forms and in several weights. They serve several functions:

✱ Prevent chafing from the uniform jersey during play

✱ Increase comfort by moving moisture away from the body to outer layers

✱ Provide an extra layer of warmth (the amount of which varies with the weight of fabric chosen)

Compression shorts, which are made of a fabric similar to compression undershirts, also are quite popular. Simply put, they prevent chafing from loose uniform shorts and provide support. Because of the support aspect, they are particularly

Donating gently used equipment

As fashion changes, your child's team changes, or your child simply grows, you will find yourself with a pile of gently used equipment. If you don't have a younger child, neighbor, or friend who can use the equipment, somewhere in the world an underprivileged soccer player would love to have it. Fortunately, programs have been popping up all over to facilitate getting your donations into the right hands. Passback is one such organization, created as a partnership between the U.S. Soccer Federation, Major League Soccer, and Eurosport.com. You can find more information at http://www.passback.org/.

popular among boys, but many girls like them as well. Like their shirt counterparts, compression shorts help manage moisture and therefore keep your player more comfortable. Expect to pay $30 or so for a pair.

Sports Bra. After Brandi Chastain's famous celebration of her 1999 World Cup winning penalty kick, how can we forget about a sports bra for girls? A soccer game involves a lot of running, so it makes sense to use a bra developed for running. Not only will it provide necessary support, but it also will help prevent chafing and manage moisture. I'm told that even young girls like to wear sports bras under a uniform jersey to allow for quick field-side jersey changes. Sports bras are widely available in a range of colors, styles, sizes, and prices ($20-$50).

SHINGUARDS

Shinguards are now recognized as such an important piece of safety equipment that they are required for play in every organized league I've ever heard of. Over the years, the style and size has changed dramatically. When I was playing in high school and college, shinguards were big clunky things that got in the way. Most of us chose certain bruises over the loss of touch that came with wearing bulky pads all over our shins and ankles, despite the protests of our parents.

Thankfully, this is a battle that parents no longer have to wage. If the kids want to play, they must put on shinguards.

ACCESSORIZING THE STANDARD UNIFORM

I haven't met a boy yet who went for uniform accessories, but the girls sure seem to. The most commonly used item is a special Velcro™ tie that keeps the jersey sleeves bunched up at the shoulder. I haven't figured out yet why girls seem to be bothered by loose sleeves when boys aren't. All I know is that I see a lot of girls using these $5 gadgets, called shirt bands or sleeve wraps. One mom points out that they make great party favors for soccer-themed gatherings.

I can, however, understand why girls are so fond of headbands and other hair-control devices. Loose, long hair and soccer don't mix. Even a light jog down the field kicks up enough wind to get a player's hair swirling annoyingly in her face. This particular accessory is not gender specific. I've known a lot of boys with hair long enough to need restraint during a game. One mom I spoke to from Fort Collins, Colorado, had a great solution for the hair-control issue. Her daughters keep a roll of stretchy athletic wrap in their bags. In addition to the obvious use as a pre-wrap under athletic tape for injuries, they pull off lengths as needed to tie hair or hold back sleeves. I think this is a great solution. It is cheap, disposable, and covers multiple uses.

What NOT to Wear

This section is all about what your player should wear. It is equally important to know what your player should NOT wear. FIFA rules and most community league guidelines prohibit players from wearing any items that may be a danger to themselves or to other players. The exact definition of dangerous is left to the discretion of the referee. Commonly excluded items are earrings, necklaces, bracelets, and casts. Check with your child's league for specific rules. If your child is tempted to wear earrings in a game or practice, keep my sister's cautionary tale in mind.

When she was in high school, her earring became caught on another player's jersey. When they separated, the earring went with the jersey, leaving a tear in her ear from the piercing to the bottom of the ear lobe. Let's just say that she not so fondly referred to that ear as Pac-Man™ until she finally had it repaired by a plastic surgeon many years later.

Most leagues require them even for training sessions. These regulations are required for very good reasons, to which I am a walking monument. I am missing a piece of shinbone even now thanks to that youthful foolishness. I should have listened to my parents!

In any case, the profile of the shinguards has become small enough that they really do not interfere with play. Had I had them available growing up, I think I'd have worn them without complaint. In fact, in one popular style, the guards are so small that one wonders (aloud and often, in my case) whether they can possibly do any good.

You can choose from a multitude of styles across a wide price range. The simplest styles for very young players start at around $10, while thin-profile, high-strength, moldable varieties cost more like $50. My in-house expert on all things related to soccer gear (my 13-year-old son), tells me that you even can buy a pair of carbon fiber shinguards specially developed to help Italian superstar Francesco Totti recover from a broken leg during the 2006 World Cup. They'd set you back a mere

$140.

Some styles include thick pads for ankle protection. I highly recommend this style for players under the age of eight. As these players are still learning to get a feel for the ball, there are a lot of misdirected kicks thrown about. By the same token, there is no touch yet to be lost via bulky ankle pads. In other words, the positives outweigh the negatives in this case. As players pick up more skill, they will naturally start to gravitate to the smaller shinguards without ankle pads. The styles using an ankle pad have a stirrup that holds the shinguards in place.

The smaller style guards must be held in place. Many come with stretchy sleeves that are worn over the shinguards, but under the socks. In the absence of the sleeves, say because one was eaten in the dryer or left on a field, the guards can be held in place with a strip of athletic tape. The shinguards go under the socks as usual, but a strip of tape is placed on the outside of the socks, below the level of the shinguards, to keep them from sliding down. The tape is replaced with each new wearing. You can find a reusable version of the same idea in the form of a Velcro™ strap.

Socks on the outside

A word to the wise for you *very* new Soccer Moms: It is a major faux pas to wear shinguards on the outside of the sock. If you send your child to practice this way, he will certainly be corrected—perhaps not so gently—by a savvier team member.

Avoiding shin itch

Remember that shinguards are worn right up against a player's very sweaty skin, which can make them bacteria safeharbors if they are not regularly washed. This can result in a mystery rash for players with sensitive skin. There are two solutions to this; either wash the shinguards regularly as you would any other gear, or consider wearing an extra pair of shinguard sleeves underneath the shinguards to protect the skin.

Soccer Ball

Technically, this is an optional piece of equipment. In most areas, the league will provide a bag of team balls to the coach for use at practice and at games. I would argue, however, that a ball is a mandatory piece of equipment. I think it is important for each child to have her own ball for use at a moment's notice in backyard games. The players with

Name that ball

Don't forget to write your family's name on the ball or it may not make its way home from the very first practice.

the best touch have grown up with a ball at their feet at nearly all times. I have to admit that it drove me crazy when my boys wanted to walk around the house with a ball at their feet, and I often sent them outside. If you can handle it, though, the constant presence of a ball is great for touch.

Soccer balls come in a variety of sizes, numbered from one (smallest) to five (largest). Sizes one and two are quite small and are not used in any league play. They are used for skill building and general backyard goofing around. You also will see these sizes used as promotional items. The exact ball size used for a given age group will be dictated by your local soccer league. As a common rule, most leagues use something close to the following age guidelines:

* **Size 3:** Very young children, usually under the age of 8

* **Size 4:** Ages 8 to 12

* **Size 5:** Ages 12 and up. Size 5 is the international competition standard as dictated by FIFA.

The ball you purchase does not need to be expensive. While your child may try to convince you that he needs a high-end ball costing in excess of $100, he doesn't. You can buy a perfectly acceptable training ball for $30 or so at your local sporting goods store, or through an online soccer specialty retailer. Another reason for not

SOCCER BALL DESIGNS

Soccer balls were traditionally made from leather with a rubber bladder, but they are now almost universally made from polyurethane (PU) with a latex bladder. A few very low-end balls are covered with PVC (polyvinyl chloride). The synthetic material now used helps minimize water absorption, which had been a major problem in the days when leather was used. What distinguishes an inexpensive ball from an expensive one? That's a good question, if you ask me, though there are those who insist that the higher-priced balls are worth the money.

Today's latest designs aim to improve the ball's energy transference (translation—the less energy the balls absorb from the strike, the more energy can be put into the ball's flight), as well as to improve the consistency and accuracy of flight. Another sought-after quality is a soft feel, which is much appreciated by those heading the ball.

There are a few things that you should look for in choosing a good solid training ball. Look for a polyurethane cover with a latex bladder. If possible, avoid balls with panels that have been glued together. Glued balls are not as durable and have a harder feel to them. Most mid-range to high-end balls are stitched. The mid-range balls are machine stitched, whereas the higher-end balls are hand-stitched.

Ball care & maintenance

Common sense goes a long way toward keeping a ball in excellent condition. If a ball gets overly muddy, give it a quick wipe down with a damp cloth, or better yet, have your player do it. Keep it pumped up to the manufacturer's recommended air pressure (usually 6 to 8 PSI). Keep in mind that balls will naturally lose air over time. Be prepared to check the pressure regularly and add air as needed. Not only is a flat or over-inflated ball more likely to be damaged, but it is also uncomfortable to play with in either case.

shelling out a lot of cash for a training ball: They have a remarkable habit of getting lost. I guarantee you that over your child's soccer career you will be buying more than one.

WEATHERPROOFING LAYERS

The length of the soccer season has been increasing over the years. Even young players often participate in two sessions of eight or more weeks each. As a result of this trend, players find themselves playing regularly in inclement weather. Make sure they have options for staying warm.

Even in relatively mild weather, it is a good idea for your player to have a warm-up suit along. Most leagues don't allow them to be worn during games, of course, but they are very useful for warming up, cooling down, time on the bench at the game, and at all times during cooler training sessions. Having one is absolutely crucial in cool weather in order to keep young players' muscles warm and prevent injury.

The suit you choose does not need to be fancy or expensive. Competitive teams usually will mandate a specific design and color for use at games, but for other kids, the suit doesn't even necessarily need to have a matching top and bottom. Your child probably already has suitable gear around that will work for training sessions and recreational games. Any sweatshirt and pair of sweatpants will do unless there is rain.

There are many options designed specifically for soccer. As you can guess by now, they tend to be made of synthetic technical fabrics that wick away moisture and dry quickly. They also tend to be stretchy and cut to fit close to the body, so as not to interfere with the player's movement. Soccer-specific warm-up suits in youth sizes usually run in the $50-$100 range. Again, a young player just starting out does not need an expensive new warm-up suit, but can get by with warm clothing she already has on hand.

If your child plays in the rain often, a set of rain gear can be a worthwhile investment. Because these suits don't tend to be as comfortable as regular warm-up suits, you probably can't get by using rain gear as an all-purpose warm-up substitute. Rain-specific jackets tend to have a loose fit and are made of stiffer, waterproof materials such as nylon.

Last, but not least, let's not forget the extremities. Keeping your child's head and hands warm on a cold day can be the difference between a pleasant and invigorating experience and a miserable one. It is not at all necessary to buy a soccer-specific hat. Any close-fitting stretch knit cap will do. It is, however, a good idea to buy gloves designed for use in soccer. These gloves are stretchy and have special grip panels on the palms that allow a player to handle throw-ins without having to take off the gloves. Gloves cost approximately $15 and are available at any soccer retailer.

GOALKEEPER GEAR

The keeper has a special role on the team, and accordingly needs special gear.

UNIFORM

Because the keeper is the only player who can use his hands, the referee must be able to identify him at a glance. For this reason virtually all leagues and levels of play require the keeper to wear a jersey that clearly distinguishes him visually from the field players on both teams. This is why you'll see keeper jerseys in shockingly bright colors. You'll also find that keeper jerseys usually have long sleeves, though they also are available in short sleeves. The long-sleeve versions have padded elbows to help soften the blow and to prevent the scrapes that can easily result from diving to save the ball. Most recreational leagues provide a keeper jersey for shared use among the various players, who usually take turns playing the position. On non-recreational teams, the keeper position generally is fixed between one or two players, each of whom usually provide their own jerseys, which start as low as $20 and can cost as much as $100.

Young and/or occasional keepers can get by with uniform shorts. Keepers who regularly play the position and who are old enough to be making diving saves often choose a padded short or pant designed especially for keepers. As with the specially padded jerseys, the idea here is to prevent the minor scrapes and bruises that can come along with the goalkeeper job.

GLOVES

Try having someone kick a ball at you full force and catch it in your bare hands. I'm quite confident you'll notice it hurts. Special goalkeeper gloves really are a necessity for all but the very youngest of keepers. The gloves are padded and serve primarily to cushion the impact of the ball. Higher-end gloves also provide a stickiness factor that helps a keeper hold on to the ball. As with the goalkeeper uniform, the gloves probably will be provided by the league in recreational divisions, while non-recreational keepers usually have to provide their own gloves. The older players usually do not mind this, as they are skilled enough by that point to appreciate having the ability to choose a glove fitting their precise preferences and fit. Many would argue that, for advanced goalkeepers, a high-quality pair of goalkeeping gloves is more important than any other piece of equipment. If you do need to purchase a pair, you will find that prices vary from under $10 for a starter youth pair to upwards of $150 for a pair designed for use in professional matches.

© ISTOCKPHOTO.COM/FOTOIE

All he needs for practice

For informal play sessions, your child need only grab her cleats, a ball, and a bottle of water to head out for a fun afternoon. For team practice sessions in warm weather, your player will need only a pair of soccer shorts, a basic T-shirt, soccer socks, shinguards and, of course, cleats.

TRAINING GEAR

The right training gear will help your player be comfortable and effective during training sessions. Keep in mind that she will participate in far more training sessions than games, so it makes sense to pay at least as much attention to what you send her to practice in as you do to game-related equipment. The equipment doesn't need to look good, but it does need to be functional.

Some, but certainly not all, non-recreational teams will issue team training shirts aimed at solidifying the team feeling. Unless that is the case, your child can and should wear any shirt that is comfortable. Don't forget, too, to send along a ball and water—both marked with your family name, of course.

When the weather gets cool, players should add at least one extra layer for top and bottom. You also should strongly consider sending your player with hat and gloves. By dressing in layers, your child will be able to shed or add layers as the training session moves through its various phases.

OPTIONAL EXTRAS

Whether or not you start to pick up some of these extras will depend upon many factors, including your child's age, playing location, skill level, and level of interest in continuing with the game:

* Running shoes—for running training that will be incorporated down the road

* Slip-on sandals—to wear to and from the field, since cleats should be used solely on playing surfaces

* Air pump—to top off the ball's air pressure as needed

* Reusable water bottle—because it's more environmentally friendly than disposable water bottles. Try stainless steel, aluminum, or BPA-free plastic bottles.

* Protective head gear—intended to greatly reduce the impact of the ball on a player's head, they cost $30-$40.

* Training aids—for backyard drills. These include small cones, an agility ladder, small goals, ball-return devices, and ball-juggling devices.

THE WELL-STOCKED GEAR BAG

If you've managed to read through the entire section on player equipment, you are probably wondering how on earth your child is going to keep track of it all when she can't even remember to take her school lunch with her on a regular basis. The answer is a gear bag. If there is a strict household rule that all equipment lives in the gear bag, and that it always should be returned there immediately after use (or after cleaning, if necessary), then you've got a fighting chance for keeping it all together. In a multi-player household, a well-organized gear bag also gives you some hope of avoiding the interminable fights over which shinguard or sock belongs to whom. Finally, if your player spends time in multiple households, as do so many kids these days, a gear bag makes it much easier to get everything to the right house at the right time.

Store it in the bag

Our household rule is that after each use, all soccer gear is to be cleaned immediately and returned to the gear bag so that it is ready to go when it is next needed. Actually storing uniforms, cleats, shinguards, and so on

in the gear bag rather than in a drawer helps avoid the last-minute frantic calls of "Mom! I can't find my blue jersey, and my ride will be here in five minutes!" This practice also means that kids will have all uniform pieces with them at all times—a major plus for those times when the team arrives at a field far from home only to find that the opposing team is wearing the same color.

Now, while that all sounds really good in theory, we've not quite managed to have this down perfectly in our house. Let's just say that it is a goal that we are working toward!

THE MAIN GEAR BAG

In order to put this idea into practice, the main gear bag needs to be large enough to accommodate all pieces of the uniform, shin-guards, warm-ups, cleats, and other small miscellaneous items. Some kids like to use a smaller drawstring fabric bag known as a sackpack, as a kind of satellite gear bag with just cleats and water for training sessions. But the larger gear bag, and everything in it, should go to all games and tournaments. That way, there is much less chance that your child will have forgotten to pack his white strip because he thought they'd be wearing blue.

Any duffle bag large enough to accommodate all of the items would do in a pinch. The soccer-specific gear bags that are available can be handy, however, because they contain separate compartments for storing cleats—a real bonus after a game on a muddy field. Some bags even have net storage pockets for carrying a ball on the outside of the bag. The choice between backpack or duffle-style bags is a matter of personal preference.

Having chosen a bag, it is time to think about what should go in it. The following list should be fairly complete, but should be personalized according to your own child's age, personal needs and tastes. As you look over the list, you'll see that it was really developed with older players in mind; six year olds will need only a few of these things.

✔ Check out the Checklist

If you are feeling really organized, you might even want to have your child keep a laminated version of his personal checklist in the bag. I'm not that organized, of course, but I've always thought it was a good idea. Come to think of it, if I had done this, we might be closer to our everything-in-the-bag-all-the-time goal!

THE WELL-STOCKED GEAR BAG SHOULD CONTAIN:

* **The full uniform strip.** If your child's team uses more than one, be sure to bring all of them along. You never know when they'll have

to make a last-minute color change.

* **Shinguards.** Carry at least one pair. Those who are charitably-minded might also carry a spare pair for the teammate who will inevitably forget his.

* **Cleats.** Players who have multiple pairs for varying field surfaces may want to carry a spare pair so that they are ready for a range of field conditions. This obviously applies only to older kids playing on travel teams. Most kids will pack a pair of firm ground cleats.

* **Base layer items.** Compression shirt and compression shorts and/or sports bra as applicable don't take up much space in the bag, but can really make the difference between comfortable and miserable if the weather takes a sudden turn for the worse.

* **Outerwear layers, if needed.** If it is cold enough that your child needs any outerwear layers, include a warm-up top and pants at a minimum, plus hat and gloves if desired.

* **Sunscreen.** Be sure to buy a formulation intended specifically for sports, because there is nothing worse than having sunscreen run into your eyes while you are playing. It also is important to use a formulation that protects against both UVA and UVB rays. If your player is anything like mine, he will resist using sunscreen while playing. Stand your ground. Skin cancer is on the rise, and most researchers think a primary cause is excess sun exposure before the age of 18. Your player will spend a great deal of time in the sun. Make sure he is protected.

* **Water bottle.** Choose a reusable model if at all possible.

* **Electrolyte drink mix.** Most sports-drink manufacturers sell small plastic containers with screw-top lids containing dry drink mix. This approach allows your player to carry many bottles' worth of sports drinks with minimal weight and to customize the strength of the drink for personal preferences.

* **Athletic tape.** This is the duct tape of the soccer world—I've seen it used to hold up shinguards, tape a weak ankle, patch up a torn shoe

or jersey, even fashion an emergency jersey number in a pinch!

* **Athletic pre-wrap.** This stretchy film is designed to go under the sticky athletic tape when taping an injured joint. It helps prevent unintended hair-waxing when the athletic tape is removed. As we discussed earlier, it also makes a handy and popular stand-in for a headband.

* **Energy bars.** By the time you figure in travel and warm-up time, your player may have to have his last pre-game meal several hours ahead. Keeping an easily digestible sports bar or two in the gear bag can help top off your player's nutritional tank just before the game.

* **Cash.** Because they've often not eaten for some time before the game, players are often starving right after the game. Keeping a few dollars tucked away in their bag means that they'll be able to buy a post-game snack, even if you're not with them.

* **Cell phone.** Before my kids reached middle school age, I used to wonder why on earth parents would buy their kids cell phones. It only took a couple of times sitting in the school parking lot for an hour waiting for the school bus to return from an athletic event with uncertain timing before I finally understood exactly why parents buy cell phones. It is for the convenience of the *parents*, not for the kids. If your child is old enough that he is participating in the odd athletic event without you (it happens, no matter how dedicated of a team follower you are), you should seriously consider providing him with a cell phone. Not only will it come in handy for arranging pick up, but it also will allow you to get the game report at the earliest opportunity!

* **Portable music player.** Optional, of course. Many older players like these for getting focused and pumped up before a game. Just look what good pre-event music did for Michael Phelps in the 2008 Summer Olympics!

* **Head band or hair accessories.** These are critical items for players with long hair—male or female—because it is important to keep hair

I.D.ing your stuff

Whatever it is that your player finally decides to keep in the all-important gear bag, make sure that you label *everything* with a permanent marking pen intended for laundry. Chances are good that at least one other player will have the exact same size and style of shinguards as your player, and I can guarantee you that they all will have the same socks and shorts. At the field kids tends to rifle through their bags, flinging gear left and right. When it all gets picked up at the end, it is very easy for one player's gear to make it into another player's bag. If it isn't labeled it may never find its way back into the correct bag. While you're at it, be sure that the bag has been labeled with at least your player's number. All of the bags tend to get dropped unceremoniously into a pile at the field, and if they are all standard team-issue and unmarked, it can take some time to sort out whose bag belongs to whom.

out of the eyes while playing.

* **Extra shoelaces.** With continued use, laces can become frayed and subject to breakage at the most inopportune times. Wouldn't it be a shame to be left out of a game for the want of a pair of shoe laces?

* **Ball.** This is an optional item, but coaches appreciate having extra balls available for warm-up. As a bonus, it also is very helpful for keeping younger siblings happy and occupied during the game.

* **Instant ice pack.** Most soccer injuries are inflammatory, which means that a quick application of ice can be very useful for preventing swelling. You can buy these packs, which remain at room temperature until activated by breaking an inner compartment, inexpensively at any drugstore. If the team carries a full first-aid kit, this may not be necessary.

FOR THE TEAM

Aside from all of the individual gear needed by each player, there are a few communal items that can make the sidelines more comfortable for the coach **and players.** Whether or not your team will want to bother with these items will depend upon the age of the kids, the size of the team, the length of the games, and how often the team travels to tournaments. Each team handles the procurement of these items a little differently. Some teams will take up a collection. Individual parents also may donate items (such as blankets or large coolers) that they already have around the house. In any case, it is nice to have a responsible parent or two bring these items rather than the coach, who already has enough to think about on game day.

* **Collapsible portable bench.** Soccer teams typically carry at least four more players on a roster than can be on the field at any one time. Players appreciate having a comfortable dry place to rest their legs between stints on the field. These collapsible benches are quick to set up and come in a carrying bag. You can find them at most specialty soccer retailers for $60–120 depending upon the number of seats.

* **Portable open-sided tent or awning.** Like the bench, this is a sideline gadget that is useful in any weather. In warm weather it provides cooling shade. In the winter it helps to keep the players and their equipment dry. Chances are good that someone on the team will already own one of these for camping.

* **Lap blankets.** When players come off the field in cold weather, their bodies cool down rapidly. Besides keeping them comfortable, it is important to keep their muscles warm to prevent injury. One or two heavy blankets spread across the laps of the players on the

bench can help keep them toasty.

* **Large water cooler.** In my opinion, players should bring their own preferred game-time drink of choice. Still, many teams opt to provide a team drink cooler.

* **Cooler with ice water and wash cloths.** When the temperature skyrockets at summer tournaments, these are a great way to cool down, providing not only comfort but also protection against dangerous spikes in body temperature. Setting this practice up is as simple as buying a large pack of inexpensive wash cloths at a big box store, then dropping them in a cooler full of ice water. Players grab one as needed to cool off. After the game, a parent volunteers to wash them so that they'll be ready for the next game.

FOR THE WELL-EQUIPPED PARENT

Yes, players need special equipment, because well, they're the players. But mom and dad shouldn't be left out either. Trust me; you will be spending enough time at the field in all seasons that you will be glad to have a few helpful items at the ready. As with your player, the exact items you choose to bring along will vary depending upon the season, whether you are headed to a game or a practice, your location and, of course your personal preferences. The lists below contain the items that I and many other moms I know have found helpful over the years. Think of them as a starting point for your own personal sideline survival kit.

THE SOCCER FAN'S LEAVE-THE-HOUSE CHECKLIST

Intrepid outdoor soccer fans must be ready for any kind of weather and to be in the elements for two to three hours at a time (more if you're at a tournament). You may want to take a clue from your player and keep all of your soccer-watching gear in a central location (such as your vehicle) to reduce the chances that you'll turn up at a game without the

The well-equipped mom

When you are headed out to take your player to practice, your needs will be a little different than for games. Unlike with games, you'll probably tire of watching practices before too long, so you'll want items to help you pass the time. You also have more flexibility regarding the weather; because you aren't necessarily watching the practice, taking refuge from the weather by sitting in the car is a feasible option. These are a few of my favorite wait-at-practice items.

* Portable music player
* Good book
* Laptop
* Extra blanket

The well-stocked minivan

Whether or not you actually drive a minivan, your vehicle can serve as a convenient location for back-up soccer necessities. Many other moms I know keep the following items in their vehicles for the duration of the soccer season so that they are ready for anything. Consider keeping your smaller soccer extras (such as sunscreen, hat, books, etc.) in a large plastic tote. You will find this approach especially convenient if you use multiple vehicles for your soccer chauffeuring duties.

* Chair
* Cooler
* Blankets
* Beach towel—to protect your seats against wet and muddy players
* Extra jackets/ coats/raingear
* Water bottles
* Snacks
* Sunscreen
* Hat
* Books/magazines
* Extra everything for the player, especially socks, shinguards, and a change of clothes
* Emergency money
* Cell phone
* Street map
* First aid kit

gear you need.

* **Chair.** If you are the type of mom who can actually sit during a game, by all means bring along a simple camp chair. I always carry one in my car, but I hardly ever use it. This may be because I'm on the petite side and can't see around the sideline pacers. Many of my fellow Soccer Moms, however, happily occupy a chair during games. If you do decide to bring one along, make sure it provides some means for hands-free carrying. Chances are that you'll need your hands for carrying the rest of your sideline gear.

* **Warm-weather items**. Sunglasses, sunscreen, a sun hat, and a sun umbrella.

* **Cool-weather items.** Hat, waterproof jacket, warm socks, and gloves. Depending upon where you live, you also may need to pull out the heavy artillery in terms of extra warm base layers. I even have a special pair of fleece-lined pants. I call these my lucky State Cup pants, because our state championship tournament takes place from January through March, and it is COLD.

* **Blanket.** Handy even in warm weather, a blanket can be used for covering up when the wind kicks up, for preventing a numb-bum if the field has bleachers, or from getting wet and

M⚽m Tip

Tools of the Trade: A few items to make your life as a Soccer Mom easier

I don't know about you, but my life has been crazy-busy for a while now. Since that fact doesn't seem likely to change any time soon—nor would I necessarily want it to—I have found a few tools that I rely on to help me manage the chaos. The first is a smart phone with calendar, task lists, email, street map/GPS system, and web capability. Because the Soccer Mom job description includes being a part-time volunteer chauffeur, I am out and about a lot. With my cell phone at the ready, people can reach me; I can catch up on my calls, manage my emails or even surf the web. Because it contains my calendar, I can check at a glance whether we are actually at the right practice field or receive a last-minute message about a change in field or location. I can even look up driving directions if I've gone astray on the way to a field (my sons would tell you that I'm severely directionally-challenged, so it happens).

I consider a wireless headset to be an essential tool to go hand-in-hand with my smart phone. If you must talk while driving (say, to ask the mom up ahead of you whether you were supposed to get off at exit 47 or 49), a headset is much safer—not to mention subjecting you to substantially lower electro-magnetic radiation.

My other survival tools of choice are a portable MP3 player and an eBook reader. I use my MP3 player to help me concentrate and drown out ambient noise when I have to catch up on work at practice or to entertain me when I'm not working. These are great for everything from simply listening to music, to learning foreign languages, to catching up on podcasts in areas of interest. I use my Kindle eBook reader to catch up on my reading.

grass stained if you must sit on the ground.

* **Water or travel mug with your favorite beverage.** Players aren't the only ones who get thirsty during a game.

* **Snacks.** You may be able to get through an entire game without nibbles, but if you've got extra soccer siblings along, you'll be glad that you can stave off any hunger-related whining.

* **Entertainment for soccer siblings.** If you plan ahead a little to keep your player's siblings entertained, you'll have a much better chance of getting to watch the game in peace.

* **Digital SLR camera or video camera.** Though it can be hard to watch a game and photograph it at the same time, it also can be great fun to have photos from across the years.

* **Phone list.** Whether you are lost when traveling to an away game, or simply need to find a ride for your child, having a team phone list handy can be a life saver. Each year, a parent on my middle son's team volunteers to create a wallet-sized laminated phone list. And each year, the rest of us parents are eternally grateful.

Camera gear for the photography-inclined Soccer Mom

Have you been taking action snap shots with your digital camera and finding the results less than stellar? If you'd like to take good action photos to document your child's soccer career, I'd recommend that you start saving up for a digital SLR camera. Regular digital cameras have a significant delay from the time the shutter is pressed until the shutter actually fires. The re-

sult? The player is often out of the frame by the time the photo has been taken. If you are really serious about getting good shots, you should also bring along a tripod or a monopod. The action moves fast and you'll need a more stable camera to keep the photos from blurring.

6 Working with Your Child's Coach

Your child's coach will be a significant fixture in your child's life, at least during the soccer season. It is best, of course, if your family's relationship with the coach is a positive one. Most of the time, it works out to be mutually beneficial and enriching for all parties concerned. Unfortunately, though, I can't say that this is *always* true. In some cases, the relationship can get a bit sticky. If that happens, it can still be a great opportunity for your child to learn to work positively with authority figures.

There are lots of ways that you can support your child's coach, even if you don't know a thing about soccer. This is particularly true if your child is playing at a recreational level, where the

coach is likely to be another parent, just like you, who is volunteering to help the kids have fun. In order to figure out exactly how you can best help the coach, however, it is useful to understand exactly what the coach's role is and what it isn't.

In this section, we'll discuss what to look for in a coach, as well as what to expect both at practice and at games. We'll talk about how you can support the coach; for that matter, we'll even talk briefly about how to *be* the coach. As with just about any relationship in the real world, you might not always agree with the coach, and that's OK. We'll suggest positive ways to handle the situation if a problem arises.

THE ROLE OF THE COACH

The job of the coach is ultimately to help players develop into individuals with the proper skills and knowledge to make good decisions during a game. Along the way, I hope that your child is also blessed with a coach who will support her personal growth and help her to have fun.

For very young players, the primary role of the coach is to serve as a friendly presence who can provide crowd control and gentle redirection toward desired activities. The ideal coach for a young recreational team, then, is a fun, friendly person who is really good with and really enjoys hanging out with young kids. Any well-meaning parent who doesn't mind a little bit of chaos can make a perfectly serviceable coach for recreational teams below the age of 8 or so.

Beyond that, the soccer knowledge required gradually increases. By the time kids hit U12 or U13 select levels, they really do need a coach with very sound knowledge of the game and preferably some playing experience. At the higher levels, coaches are depended on to construct effective practices, manage game strategy and to lead players in their individual development.

Even if a coach wanted to dictate every move during a game, the reality is that play moves too fast. Instead, the coaches should be focusing on giving the players the necessary skills in practice to make those decisions for themselves. By game time, it is too late. At the game, the coach needs to be focusing on substitution and on noting where players need more work in future practices. It is not at all practical to be trying to teach during a game. It is fine to instruct players on the bench to some extent (though they should be allowed to watch their teammates).

The coach should work with and develop *all* of the players on the team. First, you cannot always tell at age eight who will turn out to be a great player at age 16. It could merely be that the player who looks strong at eight does so because she is at the older end of her age group for the team and is larger and more developed. Second, a team is only as strong as its weakest player. It is, therefore, to everyone's advantage that all players be developed.

What to Look for in a Coach

What qualities make up an ideal coach? The exact answer is, of course, different for each player and may change as the player gets older; some players, for example, do well with authoritative coaches, while others blossom under coaches with loose, fun styles. Through the years, I've heard the opinions of many other parents on this subject, read many coaching books and researched expert opinions. Everyone has their own ideas, but the consensus seems to be that a fantastic coach will:

✱ Truly enjoy working with kids.

✱ Teach, model, and require respectful behavior, fairness and sportsmanship. This is very important for the development of the kids, but it can't hurt to serve as a great example for the parents on the sidelines too.

✱ Understand and follow age-appropriate developmental guidelines.

✱ Be fundamentally positive and approachable.

✱ Have a keen eye for each player's strength and weaknesses and, even better, have a knack for helping a child play to strengths and shore up

When you're both the coach and a parent

As moms we're used to wearing many hats. This is never more true if you happen to be both coach and parent. You have a fine line to walk between providing your player all the support she needs, while also refraining from showing any favoritism. In fact, in my experience, parent coaches tend to go toward the opposite extreme. They are so anxious not to be perceived as playing favorites that they will in fact give their own player fewer advantages than the average player. The best bet is to try to forget, just during the span of the game, that you are the parent, and just be the coach. Do your best to:

∗ Treat all children equally and with respect, including your own.

∗ Avoid singling out any child in front of the group, but be especially careful to avoid singling out your own child.

∗ If possible, try to make sure your child has other completely partial fans at the game to cheer her on.

∗ And last but not least, when all is said and done, remember to leave the game at the field. When you are at home, it is time to put the parent hat back on.

weaknesses in a *positive* way.

∗ Encourage players to take risks and experiment, giving them the confidence to do so by accepting mistakes as part of the necessary process of development.

∗ Know when to actively instruct and when to let the kids work out a lesson on their own. One of the most important skills in soccer is individual decision making on the field. If the coach always directs from play to play, the kids never have the opportunity to learn this lesson.

∗ Develop a rapport with parents and players.

∗ Be a good communicator with the players at a minimum, but ideally with parents as well.

∗ Be organized, but not so much that there is no flexibility.

✱ Have strong soccer knowledge, preferably with the appropriate formal training and certifications. A strong background as a player is nice too, particularly because it allows the coach to demonstrate proper skills.

These are all *desirable* qualities for a coach at any age, but for kids younger than age 11 or so, you should look much more closely at a coach's personal qualities and not worry so much about soccer qualifications. As the kids get older and the level of competition rises, soccer qualifications also become important. Keep in mind that the perfect coach does not exist.

COACHING CERTIFICATIONS AND LICENSES

Not all coaches carry a license, but if your child's coach does, it means he's had significant additional training—*really* significant in some cases. Better trained coaches, generally speaking, are better able to foster player development, especially beyond the recreational level. Many local leagues make informal coaching seminars available to their volunteer coaches. In addition, the U.S. Soccer Federation has a national coaching certification program intended to fill the need for consistent high-quality coach development. U.S. Soccer's basic program is progressive, starting with the introductory level E Certificate and moving toward the rare and very difficult-to-achieve National A License.

THE ROLE OF THE ASSISTANT COACH

Some teams are fortunate enough to have both head and assistant coaches. In some cases, the two coaches function as equals, using a completely collaborative approach. This can be a great approach if the two coaches have similar backgrounds and are each qualified to be a head coach, but don't want to take on the full job for whatever reason, much like job

Coaching Certifications and Licenses

Designation	Target Group	Prerequisites	Requirements
E Certificate	New recreational coaches	None	18-hour course, usually offered through state soccer associations
D License	Recreational coaches and coaches of younger select teams	E Certificate or several years playing or coaching experience.	36-hour course
National C License	Coaches of select teams, primarily for ages U12-U15	Minimum 18 years of age, must have held D license for at least 12 months (D License requirement can be waived with coaching and high-level playing experience.)	9-day course comprised of approximately 25 hours in the classroom and 45 hours on the field. Licensees must pass a written and oral exam.
National B License	Coaches of competitive teams from U16 through college	Minimum 19 years of age, must have held National C License for 12 months (C License requirement can be waived for players with 5 years of coaching experience PLUS 5 years playing at national team or Professional levels.)	9-day course, comprised of approximately 20 hours of classroom work and 48 hours of field work. Licensees must pass a difficult written, oral, and practical exam covering a number of subjects.
National A License	Coaches of elite, older teams, college coaches and national team coaching staff	Minimum 21 years of age, must have held B license for a minimum of 12 months (or as long as 3 years if the license holder did not achieve a high B-level exam score). No waiver of the B license requirement is available.	9-day course, comprised of approximately 30 hours of classroom time and 40 hours of field work. Licensees must write a paper and pass a difficult written, oral, and practical examination covering a number of subjects.

sharing.

More often, however, the second coach functions as an assistant. While the head coach has the final say on team planning, development and strategy, he will often get a great deal of input from the assistant coach, whose job it is to act as a sounding board. The assistant coach also serves as a helping hand at practice, directing drills and offering input to players. Players sometimes find it less intimidating to communicate with the assistant coach than with the head coach. Perhaps it is the perceived lower level of authority. Whatever the reason, this can be a useful communications channel for all concerned.

Coach's Gift

It is traditional for the team to buy the coach(es) a small gift at the end of the season. In my experience, that has been true whether it is a paid or a volunteer coaching position. While you may very well be tired of paying for things at the end of the season, keep in mind that a coach puts in many hours for the benefit of the team. Even if a paid coach, the good ones still put in more hours than they can be properly compensated for.

If there is a team celebration, the gift is usually presented by a parent (team manager) or by a player (the captain would be a good choice). If there isn't a team celebration, the gift can be presented at the last game. The team manager or another volunteer parent usually quietly takes up a collection at games or practices. Some teams ask for volunteer contributions in any amount an individual family feels is suitable. Other teams simply ask for a defined amount, perhaps $5-$10 per family. A $10 contribution per player on a 15-player team allows for a $75 gift for each of two coaches. If the parent in charge knows the coach well enough, a personal gift is great. Otherwise, it is common to offer the coach a gift certificate of some kind.

How the Coach Determines Positions & Substitutions

Managing substitutions during a match can be a simple matter of changing kids out on a pre-determined schedule, or it can be a complex set of strategies carefully determined with great skill as the game unfolds. When you are tempted to complain about the amount of playing time your player is getting, or disagree with his field position, remember that the coach has a lot to keep track of. When deciding when to substitute players, a coach must keep many things in mind:

* Giving each player adequate time for his own development

* Keeping the team competitive

* Balancing the play of the team as a whole (some groups work better in combination than others)

* Saving enough fresh legs to get through the whole game

* Giving players experience at a variety of positions

At the recreational level, where coaches have some responsibility for ensuring relatively equal playing time, some coaches find it helpful to create a pre-planned substitution grid. When I coached at the recreational level, I put together a simple spreadsheet template. Before each game, I'd spend a few minutes to create and print the starting line-up and substitution plan for that game. Because each game's plan was saved in the spreadsheet file, I didn't have to rely on memory to make sure that everyone was getting fair playing time and experience at all of the positions; I could easily look back across what I'd done in previous games. This approach also makes it easy for a parent to stand in as coach if necessary.

At more competitive levels of play, coaches will usually just plan out the starting line-up. Equal playing time doesn't necessarily enter into the equation, and players aren't being evenly rotated between all positions. For these reasons, substitutions are usually decided on-the-fly according to what's going on in the game at any given moment. Important considerations include who is playing well, who is hustling, who is outmatched by their opponent, or who simply needs a rest.

FOSTERING A POSITIVE RELATIONSHIP WITH THE COACH

In my experience, most coaches are drawn to coaching because they like working with kids and are good with people. As a result, they tend to be pretty easy to get along with. Just in case, though, there are a few things you can do to make sure that the relationships the coach has with both you and your child get off on the right foot.

Mom Tip

What if You are Coach for the Day?

If the day you are asked to coach is a practice day, follow the suggested no-fail practice outline later in this section. If you're asked to run a game, it is even easier. If you need to, review *At the Game* so that you'll know what to expect. Ask the coach for her line-up and substitution plan, and carry it out as best you can. It'll be fine. Really.

As with any relationship, it helps to begin with an attitude of respect and open communication. Assume, until you have reason to believe otherwise, that the relationship will be positive. In other words, be sure to give the coach the benefit of the doubt. If he does make a mistake (and he will, because he's human) try to remind yourself that he's probably trying his best. It can take some time to get to know one person, let alone a whole new team of players, so make sure to give him some time to get settled in as the coach. At the very least, remember that he is taking time out of his schedule, quite possibly unpaid, to try to help your child be a better player and a better person. That should entitle him to some leeway if you ask me.

Dr. Joel Fish points out in his book *101 Ways to Be a Terrific Sports Parent* that parents already have a model for creating a positive relationship of this type. It is helpful to think about interacting with a coach in much the same way that you would interact with your child's teacher. I think this makes sense because the coach is a kind of teacher; she is a (usually) trained specialist who is trying to help your child learn important new skills. Hopefully, you would start out by giving your child's teacher the benefit of the doubt and trust that she has your child's best interest at heart until proven otherwise. You should extend the same courtesy to your child's coach as well.

Think of this model, too, when it comes to interaction at practice or at a game. You wouldn't show up in the classroom, interrupting a lesson, to argue right then and there how it should be taught. Instead, you would probably call the teacher to arrange a time to discuss the issue privately, whether in person, by phone, or via email. Why not follow the same approach with a coach? If you've got a problem, show the coach some respect and ask to schedule a discussion.

WHAT TO DO IF YOU DISAGREE WITH THE COACH

At some point in your child's soccer career, you or your child or both are bound to disagree with a coach. When that happens, it needn't be traumatic and can even serve as a great lesson in self-advocacy for your child. Most issues are simply cases of miscommunication that are easily resolved.

In this day and age of scary, over-the-top sports parents, my first advice is to take a step back and remember that this is a *game* we're talking about. Give yourself a cooling-off period and advise your child to take the same. It could very well be that away from the excitement of the game, you realize that there really isn't all that much to talk about. If you still feel that there is a problem, ask yourself first whether this is something between your player and the coach. If so, encourage your player to speak for herself. Doing so can be a great life lesson. It is a good idea to help her develop comfort with approaching the coach and to come up with talking points ahead of time. Help her to figure out appropriate timing for the discussion (hint: NOT when the coach is busy with other players), and remind her that she'll be likely to get a better outcome if she approaches the situation with an attitude of respect.

If your child can't resolve the problem on her own, or if it isn't a player-coach issue, your next step should be to arrange to talk to the coach directly. In the vast majority of cases, the coach probably has a very good reason for doing whatever it is she's doing—she simply hasn't managed to communicate it sufficiently to you. A nice, calm, civil talk is usually enough. When in doubt, try to give the coach the benefit of the doubt. Remember that she is juggling the needs of not just your baby, but approximately 14 other parents' babies and the overall team's success at once. It is tricky.

If, after your very best, grown-up efforts, you still have an unresolved difficulty with a coach, your next stop should be the club's director of development (if there is such a position) or board. All clubs should have established procedures for grievances. Several experts recommend that it can be very helpful to have team parents approach the board as a group. The group approach gives credence to the claims, as well as removes any fear that your child will be singled-out if you speak up.

PRACTICES

When you think about soccer, you probably picture a game with its colorful uniforms, referees and cheering crowds. Most of your child's soccer experience, though, will be associated with training sessions, also called practices. This is where all of the team's coach-led learning should take place.

Practice not only leads to direct skill improvement and increased fitness levels; it also provides a risk-free environment for players to try out new moves and skills that may not be ready for prime time use in a game. Especially during the younger years, practices should focus on teaching kids the fundamentals of soccer, which is largely associated with individual control of the ball and decision making. Surprised to hear that soccer involves so much creativity? Don't be. It is one of the most critical parts of the game, and one that should be encouraged early and often at practice sessions.

HOW PRACTICE WORKS AND WHY THEY DO IT

The length and objectives for practices vary dramatically—as they should—by age group. At all age groups, however, the same general format is followed. A well-designed typical practice would work something like this:

* As kids begin straggling into practice, they will be asked to grab a ball and start working on individual skills. Young players may simply run around chasing each other, while older players will work on

What is the role of the parents at practice?

This is somewhat of a trick question. Parents don't have any role at practice, unless they have been asked by the coach to help run a drill. You can feel free to stay and watch or to leave. If you do choose to stay and watch, please don't interfere until you are asked (or, of course, unless you see something that is dangerous for players).

their juggling skills.

✱ Once the entire team has arrived, the coach will gather players for a short warm-up run and stretching. This segment may be very short—only 10-15 minutes, but is important for injury prevention.

✱ Once they are limber and ready to go, players will be divided into groups for small-sided drills. It is common for each practice to have a theme. One practice may be focused on general defensive skills, while another may focus on shooting on goal, and yet another may be geared toward developing fitness.

✱ Most practices at all age groups end with either small-sided or full-field practice games or scrimmages. If you were to poll 1,000 players, 999 of them would tell you this is their favorite part of the session.

PRACTICE DOS

According to the U.S. Soccer Federation's free publication, *Best Practices for Coaching,* practices for young players should be all about trying to emulate the informal pickup games *(street soccer)* that made so many famous players what they are today. In other words, when kids are getting started, coaches should get them together, give them a ball and an appropriately sized field; and let them go have fun. At the early ages, there should be little to no emphasis on positional play or team organization. Young players need the opportunity to experiment and work on individual skills in a free-form, fun, relaxed environment. Practices should be centered around the players—player development and player fun—not adult ideas about who should be doing what when.

As they progress in age, and are ready for more organized, well-defined play, practices also must become more organized and well-defined. But even when teams become well-oiled practice machines, free play still should form a significant portion of each practice session. Please see *Age Level Guidelines* for specific recommendations for each age level.

Getting help from older players

If you know an older, more experienced player, try to encourage her to volunteer to help in practices for younger players. Having a talented youth player to look up to can be inspiring for young players. On the flip side, the opportunity to mentor younger players is equally beneficial for the older player. I've also found that these player-coaches are infinitely less prone to lecturing than adult helpers, and they are more likely to just get out there, be goofy, and have fun. I've had my older sons help coach my youngest son's team on many occasions, and it has been a good experience for all of us. So what's the best way to make use of a player helper? Use her as a neutral player during scrimmages. Have her wear a pinnie and be on whichever team has possession of the ball. You can limit her playing in some way— say by limiting the number of touches, or allowing her only to pass. Having her involved helps each side keep possession of the ball just a little bit longer, allowing them to see and feel how more advanced play will develop. It is sort of like how reading aloud with a young student helps them experience books that are just a tad more advanced than they could manage on their own. Another way to use an advanced player helper is to have her demonstrate drills or skills.

WHAT IF YOU HAVE TO RUN A PRACTICE?

Do you have to stand in for the coach on short notice and don't know a finishing drill from a defensive drill? Don't panic. You can always fall back on the following simple formula, which will work for any age group in a pinch:

* **Warm-Up:** Spend the first 10-20 minutes of the allotted practice time in a fun and age-appropriate warm-up activity, such as tag, a passing game, or individual juggling. Follow this with a few minutes of group stretching. When I coached, my teams often asked to play a quick game of what we called hand-ball. It is like soccer, except that the ball is thrown with the hands, and no player can take more than one step while in possession of the ball. It fosters teamwork, support, and use of space, but the kids just think it's a fun game.

* **Play:** Remind yourself that the game is the best teacher so that you won't worry too much about not having an elaborate training plan. Let the kids play in some form of a low-key practice game. There are lots of variations on this. For example, you might try splitting the team into four teams and running two simultaneous small-sided games, rotating teams every 10-15 minutes.

* **Cool-Down and Recap:** About 5-10 minutes before the end of practice, call the team in to discuss observations from the game and make any necessary announcements. Afraid that you don't know enough about soccer to make any useful comments? No problem. Just ask the kids what they observed. You'll be amazed at how much they have to say! To improve their flexibility and to keep them from getting fidgety, lead them in a few simple stretches while you chat.

Practice Don'ts

When I coached my first team many years ago, a more experienced coach wisely advised me to avoid the three L's—lectures, lines, and laps—at all costs. The single fastest way to turn practice sessions from great fun to a big chore is to put kids through boring drills that require them to stand in lines. A well-designed practice will keep the kids moving, active, and engaged. The game is the best teacher. The job of the coach is to set up situations in practice that will simulate game situations. Lessons should be taught in context, rather than in a lecture format.

Just because adult soccer looks organized doesn't mean that kids are ready for that. Before the individual players on a team can work together, they must first become comfortable with their own skills, creativity, and decision-making ability. They should NOT simply be told where to go and what to do in every imaginable situation. They should be allowed to experiment and learn those lessons in a natural way.

Other than possibly as a brief part of a warm-up, laps are to be avoided because they are associated with punishment and drudgery. Running has a huge part in soccer, and players definitely need to get in some running training, but why not sneak it in as part of a fun game? Finally, the coach's focus should not be on winning at ages under 14. Instead, it should be all about individual player development.

Age Level Guidelines

You can find many books on how to run practice sessions for youth soccer players. Each will have its own opinion about the appropriate structure and focus at each age group. One of the best that I've seen is *Best Practices for Coaching Youth Soccer.*

It is concise, well-written, and available free from *USSoccer. com*. One of its clearest messages is that the coaches need to keep age-appropriate development firmly in mind: "From a developmental standpoint, the young ages are the best ones for learning skills. Spend the time now encouraging this growth. By the age of 17 the capacity to pick up new motor skills begins to wane, while the ability to conceptualize team organization, tactics, and strategy increases. As a coach, work with these strengths, not against them."

When you use this chart, be sure to take these recommenda-

Practice Guidelines

Age Group	Length	Kid to Ball Ratio	Proportion of Free Play	What They Should Be Working On
U6	30–45 minutes	1:1 or 2:1	100%	Fun, unstructured play that happens to include a ball, no discussion of positions or team concepts
U7-U8	45–60 minutes	1:1 or 2:1	80%	Individual, basic ball skills, development of coordination, directional changes, etc., still no discussion of positions
U9-U10	60–90 minutes	2:1 or 3:1, enough that everyone can interact with the ball at any time	30%++	Expanding creativity and confidence with the ball, building comfort with the ball, introducing decision making and team work
U11-U12	90–105 minutes	3:1	30%++	Individual ball skills, individual and small group decisions, exploring positional play, keeping track of other players on the field, attacking and defending

Age Group	Length	Kid to Ball Ratio	Proportion of Free Play	What They Should Be Working On
U13-U14	90–120 minutes	3:1	30%++	Team play, fitness, mental aspects of the game, developing positional play, but encouraging players to try all positions, emphasis on decision making, introducing themed practice sessions working on a particular game element
U15-U16	90–120 minutes	3:1	20%	Focus on team play, developing rhythm and flow, increased speed of play, precise control of the ball
U17-U18	90–120 minutes	3:1	20%	Fine-tuning individual skills, game insight, fitness, attitude, development of soccer sense, match preparation, game management, ability to think critically on the field

tions for what they are—guidelines rather than facts set in stone. Each player will develop at his own pace, and, therefore may have a soccer age that is slightly above or behind his chronological age. In particular, I've observed that the younger siblings in soccer families tend to have a much more sophisticated understanding of the game than their average age-group peer. When you consider all of the hours that younger soccer siblings spend immersed in higher levels of the sport, it is no wonder.

7 Playing Safe

If there is one thing that we Soccer Moms do well, it is worry about the safety and happiness of our kids. Like any kind of active endeavor, soccer is not without its potential risks. While you can't prevent all accidents, this section will tell you what you need to know to help maximize your child's health and safety—at least while she is playing soccer.

We'll start by discussing general strategies for injury prevention. We'll then move on to an overview of the most common soccer injuries. In each case, we'll tell you what to look for, how to prevent it, how to treat it, and when to see the doctor. But it isn't only injuries that you have to look out for. We'll prepare you for dealing with various field surfaces you may encounter. We'll also discuss what may be one of the most important top-

ics of all—keeping your player properly fed and hydrated. I am sure that you already know how to feed your child—she's still alive, right?—but athletes, even very little ones, have additional different nutritional needs. We'll also share a few practical tips for helping you get them the right nutrients in quick and convenient ways (for more dish on feeding your kids well in a crazy world, be sure to check out the next title forthcoming in the *For Moms* series, *Dinner for Busy Moms!*).

SOCCER IS A PHYSICAL SPORT

The risk of injuries in soccer falls somewhere between American football and chess club.

Let's put it this way: there isn't so much risk of injuries that extensive padding is required (as in American football), but there is no mistaking that soccer is a physical **sport.** Even without the contact and flying objects, a player can be injured simply by rolling an ankle. Don't hide your child in a closet just yet, though. The risk of injuries in soccer is minimal compared with many other sports, and small compared with the benefits of the active participation. The good news is that with a little bit of prevention, you can further ensure that the inevitable injuries will be kept to mere bumps and bruises.

Will my child get hurt?

In a word, yes. The question is only how badly. Sounds a bit harsh, I know, but I'm afraid it is the truth. Before you swear off soccer altogether, remember that minor injuries are a fact for just about any form of activity. They're a fact of life, really. With the proper equipment and precautions, however, you can maximize the chances that the worst injuries you'll have to deal with are a few bruises. Besides, kids are so resilient, they practically bounce. He'll be fine. Really.

Preventing Injuries

The very best way to treat an injury is to prevent it in the first place. The ultimate in injury prevention for any sport is to make sure that the player's body is strong, flexible, and healthy *before* she steps onto the field. Much of the preventative work will have to come from the child, of course, but you can help, as always, by guiding her in the right direction.

Use the Right Equipment

Soccer equipment isn't just about looking good and playing better. It is also about preventing injuries. The role of shinguards in preventing bumps and bruises in the shin area is obvious, but did you know that having a well-fitting pair of cleats is also important for injury prevention? Without the traction provided by the right kind of cleats, it is easy to slip unexpectedly, which can easily lead to muscle strains and sprains. Finally, warm-up clothing and compression articles help keep the muscles of benched players warm until they go in.

Warm Up Properly

Be sure that your child knows from a very early age that there aren't any shortcuts when it comes to warming up. Starting to play at full speed with a cold body is one of the surest ways to get an injury. This is true even for very young, strong, flexible and otherwise fit players. A proper warm-up should start with very low-intensity activity, such as a light jog, followed by stretching, and then gradually increasing activity. Most teams have this part down.

The trouble often comes in with players coming off the bench. They think that the team's pre-game warm-up is enough. It isn't. Coaches should give players a few minute's warning before they go into the game. During this time players should start by jogging slowly back and forth along the sideline, followed by stretching. Once they are warmed up, you'll often see older players work up to running a few sprints along the sideline. If the substitution opportunity still hasn't come up by that time, they should stay warm by juggling or grabbing another player to pass with. If for some reason a player has to go into a game without any warning (say, to replace an injured player), she should take care to avoid any all-out sprints or extreme twisting motions in the first few minutes. This is easier said than done—there's a game on after all!—but it is important. Many, many muscle strains are the result of an inadequate warm-up.

Stay Flexible

Stretching is a great way to prevent injuries. It is so important, in fact, that it should be thought of as a critical habit, as much a part of soccer training as dribbling or running. Think of stretching like getting a regular oil change and lube job. Soccer's heavy emphasis on running means that muscles tend to contract during the game. Without proper stretching, those muscles will start to lose their range of motion, which can, in turn, cause joint strain and, over the longterm, injury. As an added bonus, stretching is also a great way to improve agility and, therefore, playing ability.

There are a lot of myths and misinformation out there about stretching. When I was growing up, we always went through an extensive static stretching routine before we did any running at all. (Static stretches are those long, slow, deep stretches, such as the classic quad stretch where you hold one foot behind you while balancing on the other foot.) We also tended to bounce during stretching. Experts now tell us, of course, that both of those practices are a mistake.

Unfortunately, not all coaches have gotten the message, and some continue to use these potentially dangerous practices from the past. Current thinking holds that it is best to gently warm up the body, say with a slow jog, before any static stretches are performed, and it is best to leave the bouncy stretches out altogether. Very light dynamic stretches, such as gentle arm circles or leg swings, before the warm-up jog won't do any harm, but are probably unnecessary. True added flexibility comes from static stretches performed regularly *after* a warm-up, or even after a full workout. It is a great idea to have your player perform some stretches after a game to keep her muscles supple and healthy.

Which stretching moves should you try? There are many moves possible, and I'd bet that you already know a great number of them. If you need additional suggestions, try asking your child's coach for a recommended routine, check out one of the many great books on the topic, or search "soccer stretches" online. When you are helping your child choose appropriate stretches, be sure to focus on the following muscle groups: hamstrings, quadriceps, calves, groin, and hip flexors.

Whatever stretching routine your child adopts, remind her to keep the following points in mind:

* Always stretch a warm body. Immediately after a game or practice is an ideal time.

* Never, ever, ever, EVER push a stretch to the point of pain. Pain is a signal from your body that there is a problem. It shouldn't be ignored.

* No bouncing!

* Remember to breathe during the stretch.

Stay Strong and Fit

Strong, stable, fit muscles are much less likely to be injured. In the past, the focus was always on lower body strength. It is still true that leg strength is very important, both for playing ability and for injury prevention. In recent years, however, it has become clear that core strength is also important for keeping soccer players injury free. The core muscles, comprising the muscle groups of the torso from the upper abdominal area, around the back and down through the hips and buttocks, are used to initiate, stabilize, and control almost all movements.

How can you best make sure that your player is strong and fit? I certainly don't suggest that you take your seven year old down to the local gym to pump some iron. Not only is that unsafe for pre-pubescent children, it is also just silly. Very serious older players may indeed decide to adopt a formal strength training program; but for most kids, fully participating in all team training sessions will often be enough.

A common-sense approach is all that you need. Make sure that your young athlete is well rested and well fed. The body can't build itself back up after a work-out unless it has proper nutrition and enough of a break. The injury-prevention aspect of general fitness is just one reason why it is so important to make sure that your child makes it to her team's practice sessions and, just as important, that she has lots of active play opportunities outside of soccer. Participation in a wide variety of activities helps her develop all muscle groups evenly, not just those that are heavily used in soccer.

Cross-Training for Soccer

General fitness and balanced muscle strength are great injury preventers. One of the best ways to help your child stay fit year-round without creating overuse injuries or spending time in a gym is to make sure he participates in a variety of active pursuits. Activities that get the heart rate up and involve speed, strength, agility and/or hand-eye coordination are good complements to soccer. The very best activity, of course, will be one that your child loves. Consider fun activities like cycling, skating, basketball, swimming, dance, gymnastics, tennis, or martial arts. In hindsight, I see that I didn't push this issue hard enough with my own kids, and I am convinced that they've had more overuse injuries than they would have otherwise had as a result.

If you suspect that strength or fitness is a problem for your child, your first step should be to seek out other fun active pursuits. (Check out the *Cross-Training for Soccer* sidebar, on the previous page, for ideas.) You can also create a program of kid-safe supplementary exercises such as plyometrics (which is a fancy way of saying jumping exercises) or medicine ball exercises, but I'd go for the fun activities that feel like play.

LISTEN TO THE BODY'S SIGNALS

Help your child get in tune with and listen to her body's signals. Make sure she knows that she can and should STOP as soon she feels pain. Pain, after all, is the body's sign that something is wrong, and she is the only one who can feel it, so she's going to have to be able to speak up for herself. This is true even in the middle of

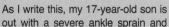

My child is out with an injury. Now what?

Though it may seem like it to your child, missing a game or two isn't the end of the world. Kids have a tendency to think they are immortal and, therefore, that they can start back sooner than is wise. Several of my Soccer Mom friends have reported that their kids (particularly older boys) get rather grumpy when they are out with an injury. As a parent, it is helpful to remember that there is an emotional side to injury rehabilitation too.

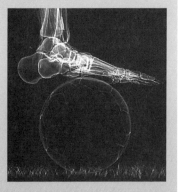

As I write this, my 17-year-old son is out with a severe ankle sprain and has to miss several of the most important games of the high school season. His tendency is to want to get back in the game as quickly as possible. I always have to remind him that there are many games to come and that it is better to let his body heal properly to prevent a one-time injury from becoming a recurring one. He continues to attend all practices and games. That way he is still in on any strategy discussions and stays connected to his team during his rehabilitation. During the first couple of practices, he merely iced his ankle. As he improved, he began to do simple drills (modified for his ankle's current condition) to start regaining strength and range of motion.

a game, no matter how important the game may seem. And by all means, if your child's coach pushes her to play through pain at any age, push back. Playing through pain is rarely a good idea. At best, it is no fun for the player. At worst, it could cause permanent damage. Be sure to browse through the section on common injuries so that you'll recognize the signs that a problem may be forming.

REHABILITATE CAREFULLY TO PREVENT FUTURE PROBLEMS

The first step in rehabilitating an injury is to understand exactly what you're dealing with. For the most common injuries, the issue at hand will be obvious. If you have any doubt at all, don't hesitate to visit your doctor. Kids are incredibly resilient, to be sure, but a minor problem improperly treated can become a major one.

See the *Common Injuries* section for an injury-by-injury breakdown, but for the vast majority of cases, getting ice on the affected area should be your first step to dealing with a new injury. Ibuprofen taken immediately from the team's first aid kit—they have one, right?—can help to ward off swelling and the pain associated with it. In the first few days, swelling is the enemy, and all initial treatment efforts are geared toward reducing it. Check with your child's doctor, but a commonly recommended course of treatment for the first 24-48 hours is the tried-and-true RICE method:

* **Rest.** Even when an active rehabilitation will be called for, the injured area should be rested completely for the first few days. If you are dealing with a lower leg injury, this may mean using crutches. You can rent a pair of these cheaply at most any drug store.

* **Ice.** Place an ice pack (see sidebar) on the affected area for 20 minutes four to eight times per day. *Don't* put ice directly on the skin; Use a dishtowel or wash cloth to wrap the ice. Also, *don't* put any heat on the area within the first few days, as it can increase swelling and pain.

* **Compression.** When your child isn't icing the area, wrapping the affected area with a compression bandage can help to keep swelling

down to a minimum.

✱ **Elevation.** When practical, have your child raise the injured area above the level of his heart. Since this is soccer we're talking about, the injured area is likely to be in the lower body, which means in turn that elevation will require lying down on a comfy couch with the injured area propped up on pillows.

Once you've made it past that crucial first day or two, it is time to think about rehabilitation. Remind your child to take it slow. Every kid I've ever known wants to get back on the field as quickly as possible. If they don't let the injury fully heal, however, it can become a nagging, recurrent problem.

Taking it slow does not, however, mean that she should necessarily stop using the injured parts at all. In fact, the current thinking is that after the first few days, controlled, gentle use of the injured area is the best road to healing. This so-called active rehabilitation allows for the injured area to retain its range of motion and muscular strength. If it is a joint that's being rehabilitated, and it often is, you can provide support during the active rehabilitation phase with either a store-bought brace or by taping the ankle. An active rehabilitation isn't appropriate for all injuries of course, but for most minor soft-tissue sprains and strains, it is just the ticket. One final word of caution though: make sure your player knows that she should stop immediately if she feels any pain.

Finally a use for those vegetables your child won't eat!

Sticking a hard block of ice on a soft-tissue injury is both uncomfortable and ineffective. You can buy soft, flexible and reusable ice packs in any drug store. With three soccer players in the house, we always have several of these in the freezer ready to go. If you have an injury on your hands and find yourself without a flexible ice pack, you've probably already got a great substitute ready to go. Simply grab a bag of frozen vegetables from the freezer (peas and corn work best).

COMMON INJURIES

When you're on the lookout for potential soccer injuries, there are two primary types to keep in mind—acute and overuse.

The most obvious type of injury is an acute one. If you can point to the moment that an injury occurred, it is acute. A concussion, for example, generally occurs from a single unexpected blow to the head. You can't see it coming, and there is no way to limit its effects by catching it early. Overuse injuries, on the other hand, occur from, well, overuse. They come on gradually over time and may only present subtle signs until they are quite developed. Shin splints are an example of this type of injury. The first sign that your child has an overuse injury will likely be a complaint of a nagging ache or pain. Take these complaints seriously because this is your chance to stop the progression of the injury before it becomes more serious.

In dealing with both types of injuries however, the first key is to identify the problem. Use this section as your quick injury cheat sheet. This information should not substitute for your doctor's or trainer's advice, but we've provided it as a reference to at least help you be on the lookout for some of soccer's most common offenders.

✚ BLISTERS

What it looks/feels like: We've all had these before. Most blisters look like tiny balloons under the skin, filled with clear fluids. Not all of them are raised, however. Watch out for them on the heel and toes, particularly during the break-in period for a new pair of cleats.

Causes: Blisters are always caused by friction. The only question is what caused the friction. Usually, a brand new pair of shoes is the culprit. Playing with wet socks can also cause problems.

Prevention: Buy new cleats early enough that they can be used intermittently with the old cleats as they are broken in. Please don't send your child off to a three-day tournament in brand new cleats. That's just asking for blisters. With blisters, an ounce of prevention is worth many pounds of cure. If your child is playing in new shoes or will be playing many more games in a shorter period than he is used to, consider using an anti-blister lubricant stick all over the foot. (Glide® is one of several commercial products available.) In the old days, we used plain old petroleum jelly, but that's a big mess. Besides, it just seems wrong to be using something with the word petroleum in it on a child's skin. You can also use moleskin pads to help keep the shoes from rubbing the feet. Another common trick is to wear two pairs of socks. (Soccer socks are awfully thick already, so the first pair should be a very thin liner layer.)

Treatment: If the skin over the blister is still intact, your best course of action is usually to leave it alone. To break the blister open would be to turn it into an open wound, which then introduces the possibility of infection. Clean the area with antiseptic soap, then apply moleskin or other foam padding around the area with a hole cut out of the middle to accommodate the blister. If you don't have any kind of pad available, a bandage can be used in a pinch, but it doesn't do as good a job of preventing further friction. A thin covering of antibiotic ointment over the blister isn't a bad idea either. If the blister is so large and swollen that it is causing pain, it can be carefully drained. Just make sure that you do so very carefully and use a sterile instrument like a needle cleaned with alcohol. Leave as much of the skin intact as possible, and proceed to treat like an open wound.

If the skin over the blister is broken, you have to be on the lookout for infection. Treat it like you would treat any open wound; apply antibiotic ointment, then cover with a sterile gauze (use athletic tape to secure the gauze in place). You can also apply a foam pad (with a hole cut out for the blister) for protection. After a few days, the skin over the blister will probably dry out and become stiff and ragged. You can carefully cut this skin away with a small pair of scissors. Don't cut the skin off right away, though, because it can help to provide an extra protective layer for the first few days as the blister is healing.

When to see the doctor: You'll see lots of blisters over the years ,and they are almost always easy to cure at home. You probably won't need to see the doctor unless you see any signs of infection, which include opaque liquid, an off-smell, or redness and swelling in the area surrounding the blister.

✚ Bruises

What it looks/feels like: You probably don't need me to tell you what bruises look like. If you've gone your whole life without getting a bruise, you need to get out more. Just for the sake of completeness, let's say that bruises look like splotches of technicolor skin that are sore to the touch and possibly slightly swollen. These could pop up most anywhere in soccer players, but are found most often on the lower legs.

Causes: Bruising is usually caused by some kind of blunt force trauma (translation: getting kicked or smacked with the ball). The trauma causes capillaries in the surface of the skin to break, allowing blood to seep into surrounding tissues. Bruising can also show up as a secondary sign of a soft-tissue injury like a sprain or a strain.

Prevention: Properly-fitting and regularly used shinguards are the best prevention for soccer's most common bruises.

Treatment: Most bruises require no treatment. They, more than just about any other of the injuries listed here, go along with the soccer territory. Your child will probably regularly have bruises when she isn't even exactly sure how she got them. If the bruise is extensive or causing discomfort, the RICE method previously described, along with some ibuprofen or acetaminophen, can provide some relief.

When to see the doctor: If the bruising is much more extensive than is warranted by the degree of the trauma, it may indicate a more serious problem. If you notice that the bruise has become firm, it might have developed into a hematoma, which might need to be drained by a doctor.

✚ SHIN SPLINTS

What it looks/feels like: Shin splints show up as pain along either the inside or the outside of the shin bone. It is possible to get these in only one of the lower legs, but it is more commonly present in both legs. The pain usually starts as a very mild ache but can become intense if ignored. Shin splints are an overuse injury, so be especially alert to them at the beginning of a season when there is more likely to have been a sudden increase in the amount of training. You can save a lot of pain if these are caught and treated early. If they aren't treated early, they can become an almost chronic issue, particularly in people whose biomechanics predispose them to it. I am one of those people, and I've had them many, many times. Believe me when I say that you should really have sympathy for your child with shin splints; they can *really* hurt.

Causes: Shin splints are generally caused by doing too much too soon, and commonly appear at the beginning of the season. While the jury is still out on exact causes, many believe that they are exacerbated by a lot of running on hard surfaces without proper arch support. They may also be exacerbated by overly stiff and inflexible calf muscles.

Prevention: The best way to deal with shin splints, of course, is prevention. Include a supportive premium footbed in cleats, and have your player change to proper running shoes for any track-based conditioning. Have her stretch properly (see *Stay Flexible*), paying particular attention to the calf muscles, and participate in pre-season conditioning in order to avoid ramping up fitness efforts too quickly. If your child is prone to shin splints, it might even be a good idea to have her pursue a course of preventative treatment during the early season; ice after practice sessions even before leg pain appears.

Treatment: Shin splints are an inflammation issue. Treat with regular ibuprofen and ice-cup massages. To make ice cups, fill a number of small disposable paper cups half full with water and freeze. After each session, have your child take a cup and tear away enough of the outer paper level to reveal ice. Massage the ice directly along the sore tissue. If caught and treated early, your player may be able to continue playing with shin splints. Once they get to the point that the pain is significant, however, they will most likely need a rest period of a week or two in order to return them to a manageable level. Because inflexible calf muscles can cause problems, it is a good idea to stretch both the front of the shins and the calf muscles after each practice. Finally, like other inflammation-related injuries, compression can provide some relief. The easiest way to get compression on the shins is to wrap them with athletic tape.

When to see the doctor: If you've been treating your child's shin splints carefully using all of the suggestions, particularly by providing proper rest and managing the inflammation, and you aren't seeing any improvement, you should see a doctor. There is a more serious condition called a stress fracture that can feel somewhat like shin splints.

✪ RASHES

What it looks/feels like: Rashes can take many forms, but the most common ones from soccer-related causes involve small red bumps on the shins.

Causes: In the case of shin rashes, the shinguards are likely to blame. Shinguards are worn under soccer socks, usually directly on the skin. This creates a tight, warm, and often sweaty environment. In other words, it is a perfect little laboratory for all manner of bacteria and fungi. In some cases, rashes could be a reaction to the material used in the shinguards. Rashes in other areas may be related to heat, moisture, and/or friction (Prickly Heat).

Prevention: Make sure all clothing and equipment is frequently washed. In the case of shinguards, they are used so frequently that it is sometimes hard to squeeze in a washing. Because they are so inexpensive, one easy solution to this problem is to keep a second pair on hand so that one pair can be worn while the other is being washed. Avoid wearing wet clothing or equipment and, if necessary, use cornstarch to absorb excess moisture. You can also try using a thin sleeve or pair of socks *under* the shinguard (you'll still want to have the soccer socks *over* the shinguards). If you suspect that a contact allergy is involved, try using another type of shinguard.

Treatment: Make a special effort to keep clothing and equipment scrupulously clean and dry, and have your child remove shinguards immediately after play. (Many kids unnecessarily leave their socks and shinguards on for hours after a game.) Given a proper airing, most rashes will clear up quickly on their own. If not, you can try over-the-counter soothing creams. You can also help absorb excess moisture by dusting any affected areas with cornstarch.

When to see the doctor: If the rash doesn't respond to the suggestions above, gets worse, or shows any signs of infection, you should have a doctor take a peek at it.

✚ INSECT STINGS

What it looks/feels like: Bee stings come with their own built-in alarm system (a wailing child), so chances are you'll know exactly what's going on, even before you see the site of the sting. Everybody reacts a little differently, but most people will get a local reaction at the site, with redness and swelling.

Causes: Crossing paths with a bee, wasp, or other stinging insect at the wrong place and time. Believe it or not, stings can happen right in the middle of practices or games, and the kids usually don't see them coming.

Prevention: Other than suggesting that you don't spray your child down with sugar water before a game, I'm not sure there's much practical prevention available. It happens.

Treatment: The very first thing you should do is check for a stinger and remove it IMMEDIATELY if one is present. It is fine to grab it with your fingers, or just scrape it off. Experts say that the severity of the reaction is in part determined by how long the stinger was left in the skin, so get it out as fast as you can.

Immediately after removing the stinger, if any, try to determine whether the victim has a known bee allergy. Take this seriously because, left untreated, bee stings in a child with a severe allergy can be fatal. If the victim does have a known allergy, he will hopefully have an epinephrine shot on hand. If he does, administer it right away using the directions that should be with it. If he is supposed to have one, but doesn't, don't send someone home to get it. There isn't time. You should call 911 instead. Do not wait until the victim is showing symptoms. While you're waiting for help to arrive, ask if anyone has any antihistamines with them. These won't substitute for emergency treatment, but they can sometimes at least help slow down the reaction.

In the absence of a known allergy, the biggest job you'll have is comforting the victim. Bee stings don't hurt for long, but they tend to be quite an unwelcome shock to the child. If the site is red and swollen (and it probably will be), applying some ice can help. You can also administer ibuprofen or acetaminophen to help with both the pain and the swelling. (Needless to say, you should be cautious when giving medications to someone else's child without a parent's consent.) Later, there might be some itching at the sting site. Over-the-counter antihistamines might help.

In the minutes after the sting, keep a close watch for any signs of an allergic reaction, especially if this is the child's first sting. Signs include extreme redness, itching, swelling, hives, and shortness of breath. The first three signs will also occur in a non-allergic child, but with less severity, so you're looking for a more severe reaction than normal. Shortness of breath does not happen at all with a non-allergic child, so if you see any sign of that, be sure to call for medical attention right away.

When to see the doctor: Seek emergency medical attention immediately if you see any signs whatsoever that the child has a bee sting allergy. And I mean *immediately,* as it can be a matter of life and death. Even with a non-allergic child, you should consider a trip to the emergency room if the child was stung many times—roving swarms don't tend to hang out on soccer fields, so this would be rare in a soccer setting—or if the sting occurred in a location where any significant swelling could cause difficult breathing, such as the mouth, throat, or nostrils.

✪ HEAT ILLNESSES

What it looks/feels like: Heat-related illnesses can range from the relatively mild and easily treatable heat-rashes to the potentially life-threatening heatstroke. According to the National Institutes of Health, you should be on the lookout for any of these symptoms of heat exhaustion, which precede heatstroke:

* Excessive sweating

* Fast, weak pulse

* Rapid breathing

If not immediately treated, heat exhaustion can progress to heatstroke. Interestingly, its symptoms are in several ways opposite those of its precursor condition:

* Dry skin

* Rapid, strong pulse

* Dizziness and/or confusion

* Throbbing headache

* Nausea

* Body temperature over 103 degrees

Causes: Heat illnesses occur when the body temperature rises too quickly and to too high of a level. This can happen when a child is exposed to high heat for too long, particularly during physical activity and/or when she is not properly hydrated.

Prevention: On really hot days, you can help prevent these dangerous illnesses in your child by encouraging her to stay out of the sun as much as possible. If she must be in the sun, be sure that she is properly hydrated and is wearing sufficiently cool clothing. Have her *drink before* she is thirsty. Consider carrying a cooler full of ice and wet wash cloths along to games and training sessions on especially hot days. Anything that can be used to lower body temperature can help prevent these serious issues from occurring.

Treatment: If you suspect that your child is suffering from heatstroke, you should seek emergency medical attention for him. In the meantime, or if your child is only suffering from heat exhaustion, you should do everything you can to immediately lower his body temperature. Begin following these common-sense steps:

✱ Get him out of the sun as soon as possible.

✱ Use wash cloths, a shower, a cool bath. Use a bucket if you need to. Just keep in mind that immersion in water is the fastest way to bring someone's body temperature down.

✱ Give plenty of fluids.

When to see the doctor: Call for emergency assistance immediately if you see any signs at all of heatstroke.

✚ SPRAINS AND STRAINS

What it looks/feels like: Though they have different names, sprains and strains feel much the same. Both involve the stretching or tearing of soft tissue; a sprain refers to an injury to a ligament (the connective tissue that joins bone to bone), whereas a strain refers to an injury to a muscle or tendon (the connective tissue that joins muscle to bone). In either case, it is usually an acute injury; the player can point to the moment that the injury occurred. They may even feel a pop or tearing sensation and will feel pain, sometimes excruciating.

Sprains and strains vary from mild to severe in intensity. In the mild cases, the soft tissue involved is merely stretched. It may cause some mild discomfort, swelling, and bruising but isn't likely to decrease the functionality of the injured area for long, if at all, and the player is usually still able to put weight on the injured area. In moderate cases, the soft tissue is partially torn, leaving the player with significant joint or muscle instability. The swelling and bruising will also be more severe. The most severe cases involve a full rupture of the soft tissue, which can leave the associated joint or muscle completely nonfunctional. Bruising and swelling will be severe and extensive. If the injury is primarily to a muscle (i.e., a strain), signs might also include muscle spasms or weakness.

Causes: Most sprains and strains are acute injuries resulting from some sudden trauma or displacement of the muscle or joint. The all-too-well-known rolled ankle is a good example. Some muscle strains, however, are the gradual result of chronic overuse.

Prevention: It is impossible to prevent all strains and sprains. Sometimes a player just happens to land the wrong way, or collides with another player. You can lessen your player's chances of a severe sprain, however, by following all of the recommendations in the *Preventing Injuries* section. In particular, making sure that your child is strong, fit, flexible, balanced, and well-nourished will go a long way toward the prevention of sprains and strains. And above all, make sure that a careful, well-thought-out warm-up precedes every training session or game. If you suspect that your child has weakened joints (particularly the ankles or knees), perhaps due to a previous injury, it is a good idea to provide extra support with athletic tape or a brace.

Treatment: Use the RICE method for the first couple of days.

Mild to moderate sprains and strains will benefit from gradual active rehabilitation. Just be sure that your player knows that she should use pain as a guide. The rule is simple: If it hurts, stop doing it! Severe sprains and strains that involve complete tissue ruptures may need to be splinted or cast. The very worst cases may even require a surgical repair. During rehabilitation, it is important to try to stay active, even if the injured joint can't be used normally. It is sometimes possible to substitute swimming or water jogging until the injured area is strong enough to be used again. The key is to help your child be patient; moderate to severe sprains and strains can take weeks to months to fully recover.

When to see the doctor: As with all things, let your judgment be your guide. Our instincts when it comes to our children are usually pretty good. If the injury seems particularly painful, or if it does not respond to treatment, it is always a good idea to seek medical attention. (If a fracture or serious injury is suspected, do not remove the athlete's socks or shinguards as they can provide protective compression.) And certainly if the injured area is completely non-functional, that is a sign that the soft tissue involved may have ruptured completely. Another issue is that some fractures may look just like a sprain in the early days.

According to the National Institutes of Health, you should take your child to see a health care provider if any of the following are true:

* Your child cannot put enough weight on the joint to walk at least four steps without significant pain

* There are any obvious visual hints of fracture, such as lumps, bumps or deformities

* Your child is unable to move the joint, or if it buckles when she tries to use it

What if my child gets hurt when I'm not there?

We'll all keep our fingers crossed that this doesn't happen, but unless you can be there for every second of practice and games, it very well could. My son once got a concussion when I wasn't there, so I know that it happens. Most injuries are minor bumps or bruises that don't require much more than some sympathy from the coach for a moment. But the adult in charge needs to be prepared to deal with the more serious issues that can come up.

The good news is that every soccer league that I've ever run across has procedures to deal with this scenario. Your league's registration procedure will almost certainly contain an emergency medical form, including your doctor's contact information, your emergency contact information, any allergies or special conditions, and insurance information. It should also contain a statement of consent for treatment. This is such an important element for your child's safety that you should supply the information even if you aren't asked for it.

Your coach or team manager should carry a copy of every player's emergency medical information to EVERY game and training session. No exceptions. She might go an entire season without needing them, but they're invaluable if any trouble should arise. One of my son's teammates broke his leg during a match while his parents were watching a sibling play. Thanks to the emergency form, another parent was able to contact his parents and get the player emergency medical treatment until the parents could arrive.

✱ Your child reports feeling numbness near the injured area *or* extreme pain

✱ You notice a red, tender, swollen area that is directly above a bony area (i.e., not around a joint, like the ankle)

✛ PLANTAR FASCIITIS

What it looks/feels like: If your child complains of heel pain, especially if it is worst when she first wakes up in the morning only to improve as the day goes on, you should suspect plantar fasciitis (unless it occurs during the early puberty years and/or is in both feet, in which case you should also consider Sever's disease, described later). Plantar fasciitis is an inflammatory condition that occurs when the plantar fascia, a thin band of tissue connecting the heel to the forefront, is injured. The amount of pain can range from very mild to severe stabbing pain. In more advanced cases, the pain can radiate from the heel up into the arch area.

Causes: Plantar fasciitis is most often an overuse issue, though it can happen acutely in some cases. Some people are just built in a way that makes them prone to plantar fasciitis. In particular, if a person tends to roll their foot inward excessively while running (called over-pronation), it can gradually put enough stress on the plantar fascia to cause the condition. It can also be the result of regularly wearing footwear with inadequate arch support. People with very high arches are particularly susceptible to this problem.

Prevention: Plantar fasciitis can be frustratingly persistent once it takes hold, so it is worth the trouble to try to prevent it, especially if you know that your child over-pronates or has high arches. It might be a good idea to use premium over-the-counter foot beds in his cleats and street shoes for extra arch support or to ask your child's doctor about prescription orthotics. Many kids have found both relief and prevention by wearing heel cups in both their cleats and street shoes. Heel cups work by raising the heel up slightly to take some pressure off of the plantar fascia.

Treatment: The RICE method works here as with other inflammatory conditions. Try adding heel cups and/or arch supports, as well as exercises that stretch the plantar fascia. In severe cases, you might consider having your child use a night splint, which is a device designed to keep the foot flexed over night in a position that takes the pressure off of the plantar fascia. It is important to be patient. Even very mild cases can take weeks to resolve. More advanced cases may take up to a year. If a case doesn't resolve after a year, it may be necessary to correct the problem with surgery.

When to see the doctor: See the doctor if your child's case does not respond to the recommended home treatment, especially if she is still experiencing any heel pain after a year.

✪ SEVER'S DISEASE

What it looks/feels like: If your child complains of heel pain and is in the pre- or early puberty years, he may very well be dealing with a case of Sever's disease. It is more common in boys, but it can affect girls too. The most common age of occurrence differs by gender. It hits at around age 10 to 12 for boys and between ages 8 and 10 for girls.

Sever's disease will usually pop up at the beginning of a season. You may notice that your child limps and starts to favor walking on his toes somewhat. It is possible for the pain to be in just one foot, but you'll most commonly see it in both feet at once. Try squeezing both sides of your child's heel at the very back. If it causes any increased discomfort, it is probably Sever's disease.

Causes: In very early puberty, the bones of the foot tend to grow faster than the associated muscles and tendons. As you might expect, this can cause the tendons to become very tight for a time. Because sports cause increased strain on the tendons, active kids are at the highest risk for Sever's disease. For some reason, it is especially common among soccer players.

Prevention: The best way to prevent Sever's disease is to encourage your child to maintain excellent flexibility in her lower legs, especially during the growing years. She should pay particular attention to stretching exercises that keep the Achilles tendon, calf muscles, and hamstrings flexible. Having her wear well-fitting, supportive shoes can help too. It is also important to avoid walking or running long distances on hard surfaces.

This is one of those cases where I sure wish I'd known then what I know now. When my youngest son was 10 years old, my husband and I took him and his brothers on a 16-day trip. Along with the rest of us, my son walked miles every day on pavement. Unlike the rest of us, though, he was wearing basic skateboarding-style shoes, which aren't exactly known for their arch support. During the last week of the trip he started to complain that his feet hurt, each day worse than the day before. At the time, we thought it was a natural result of all that walking. When we got home, however, we found that the problem continued. And when soccer season started the very next week, it only got worse. Before too long, it got so bad that he could hardly walk without a limp, and we went to see our doctor, who diagnosed it as Sever's disease. Through treatment, we were able to get the symptoms to the point where they were manageable (barely), but it was a full 18 months before they went away entirely.

Treatment: Most cases of Sever's disease resolve on their own as soon as the player's growth slows down a bit. With that said, it isn't terribly comforting to a child suffering from the condition to tell him, "Don't worry, it'll clear up in a year or two." Unfortunately, that's about the truth. The good news is that there is no long-term damage associated with the condition.

If the case has become severe, like my son's, your child should rest completely for a couple of weeks. During that time, apply the RICE method two or three times per day. You can give him ibuprofen for the pain and to help manage the inflammation. When he's ready to start back, consider having him use arch supports or heel cups, and continue with the icing regimen.

When to see the doctor: You might want to see the doctor if you aren't sure whether it is Sever's disease, plantar fasciitis, or some other cause that is creating the heel pain. Be sure to check with your doctor if the pain doesn't at least improve with treatment. (Don't expect it to go away completely right away, because it probably won't.)

✚ Osgood-Schlatter Disease

What it looks/feels like: This, along with Sever's disease, has got to be one of the most common injuries that you've never heard of. According to some experts, Osgood-Schlatter disease may affect as many as one in five young athletes. As he goes through the growth spurts of puberty, your child may experience a painful lump under one or both knees. Osgood-Schlatter is more common in boys, but it can affect girls too. The most common age of occurrence differs by gender. It hits at around age 13 to 14 for boys and between ages 11 and 12 for girls.

The pain associated with Osgood-Schlatter disease ranges from very little to severe. In most cases, it will increase with the amount of activity. The pain either may be relatively constant during your child's rapid growth phase or may come and go. Either way, it will likely disappear on its own once your child has stopped growing.

Causes: Osgood-Schlatter disease is caused when heavy participation in sports with running, jumping and bending creates stress on the tendon that connects the kneecap to the shinbone. During the rapid growth phase, these stresses create additional stress on the already-sensitive growth plate, which leads to painful swelling and tenderness below the knee.

Prevention: Because it is the quadriceps that are placing the extra stress on the knee tendons, it may help to keep those muscles extra strong and flexible.

Treatment: Most cases of Osgood-Schlatter disease resolve on their own as soon as the player has stopped growing. The standard treatment of inflammatory conditions applies here as well: try the RICE method. You can use ibuprofen as necessary to manage pain, but consider that a rest or a brief switch to sports that do not involve running, jumping, or bending (such as cycling or swimming) may be in order.

If my child gets hurt should I get angry at the coach or sue?

Except in cases of very clear and severe negligence by the coach (circumstances that I have never seen and have trouble even imagining), no, you should not be angry. Bumps and bruises are part of life, and they're certainly part of soccer and other sports. Virtually all soccer injuries happen during active play. Even when there is some fault involved, it would be the fault of another player—a juvenile—and not any adult that you could or should sue. (Don't get me started on how stupidly litigious our country has become.) The question of fault with respect to soccer injuries is a very fuzzy one.

When to see the doctor: It is a good idea to see a doctor when your child first displays symptoms of Osgood-Schlatter disease so that she can rule out other, potentially more serious knee conditions. You should also see a doctor if the treatment methods aren't helping the condition.

✚ Concussions

What it looks/feels like: As an acute injury, you and your child will almost certainly be aware that a potential head trauma has occurred, so you will know to be on the lookout for the symptoms of a concussion, which include:

* Severe headache and/or dizziness

* Nausea and vomiting

* Confusion and/or amnesia

* Ringing in the ears

* Slurred speech

* Sleepiness

* Impaired balance

* Visual disturbances

* Pupils that are dilated or unequal size

Causes: Concussions can be caused by blows to the head that cause the brain to hit forcefully against the skull. In soccer, potential causes of concussion include heading a hard

Is there insurance?

I suppose I can't speak for every league out there, but I can say that leagues have too much potential liability NOT to carry insurance for injuries sustained during league events. The exact coverage differs from league to league, but in any case, it will only cover injuries that happen during an official team practice or game. It is also usually secondary to any other insurance you may have. If you've already got good health coverage for your child, you really don't need to worry about this at all. If you DON'T already have good coverage of your own, it would be a great idea to make sure that the league's coverage is sufficient and in force.

THE SOCCER FIRST AID KIT

The first aid kit that you use for soccer will be very similar to your general first aid kit. You can take the easy route, as our family did, and purchase a pre-packaged first aid kit or put together your own. Whichever option you choose, make sure it includes the following items at a minimum:

* Ibuprofen
* Adhesive bandages in various sizes and shapes
* Instant ice pack
* Athletic tape
* Blister-treatment supplies
  (ointment and Band-Aids or moleskin)
* Sterile gauze
* Antiseptic wipes

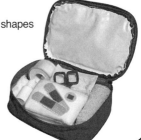

ball incorrectly, bumping heads with another player, and running into a fixed object (like a goal post).

Prevention: Short of wearing head gear or refusing to head the ball, there isn't much that you or your child can do to prevent a concussion. Even then, concussion is still possible from a collision with another player or a fixed object.

Treatment: For all but the most serious cases requiring surgery, treatment for a concussion consists of rest and over-the-counter medications to manage the associated headache. Rest is the most important part. The brain is fragile while healing. If your child were to play again too soon and receive a second concussion before the first was healed, the damage could be far more serious and long-term. If your child has a concussion, expect him to be sidelined for at least one to two weeks.

When to see the doctor: It is wise to at least call, and preferably to see, your child's doctor any time you even suspect a concussion. Needless to say, head injuries can be extremely serious. This just isn't an injury you want to mess around with.

SPORTS NUTRITION AND HYDRATION

Feeding your young athlete well is one of the most concrete actions you can take to reduce his likelihood of injury, his ability to perform well in the game, and his capacity for having fun.

When we look at it this way, it is hard to ignore the importance of proper nutrition and hydration. Fortunately, if you keep just a few guidelines in mind, you'll see that feeding and hydrating your child well doesn't have to be time-consuming, difficult, or expensive.

GENERAL GUIDELINES

Ultimately, the specific foods that you give your child to eat will have to depend upon your own family's needs and taste preferences. For this reason, I'll stay away from advising specific foods and instead offer a set of guidelines compiled from a variety of nutritional experts.

* First and foremost, it is important to remember that young athletes are not mini adults. They are still growing and as such have special nutritional needs. For example, young athletes should have a diet higher in carbohydrates than most adults. Make sure that you and your child are accounting for the greater caloric needs that are due to both growth and to the extra athletic activity.

* The American Academy of Pediatrics recommends that youth athletes take in 50-55% of their calories from carbohydrates, 20-35% from fats, and 15-20% from proteins.

* Variety is important. It important that your child eat lots of different types of foods and not too much of any one kind. Yes, carbohydrates provide immediate energy, but protein and fats have important roles to play too. The key in this, as in all things, is moderation and balance.

* For strong, healthy bones, the American Academy of Pediatrics also recommends making sure that your child's calcium intake is 1,200-1,500 mg. per day. Great sources of calcium include the obvious dairy sources like milk, cheese, and yogurt. But did you know that spinach is also an excellent source of calcium?

* Unless your child's doctor has identified that she has special nutritional needs, supplements are not necessary and some may even do some harm. Your child will be much safer getting the needed nutrients from nutritious whole foods. In any case, please check with a doctor before you allow your child to even consider any supplement other than a children's multivitamin.

* No meal skipping. Period.

* Snacking is a good thing. Just make sure the snacks involve

Eating Well on the Road

Fast food can be healthy away from home. Good choices include sandwich shops, pizza (with caveats: thin crust and veggie toppings are much better than thick crust and pepperoni), and salad bars. If your travel includes time on an airplane, remember that flying is exceptionally dehydrating. Have your child carry a bottle on board and drink frequently. Don't rely on the airline's occasional small cup of soda. It won't be enough to ensure that your child is adequately hydrated for athletics. While she's at it, it is also a good idea to bring along snacks to keep energy levels going.

WHAT TO EAT FOR AN EARLY MORNING GAME?

Soccer schedulers love their early morning games. Many regular season games start as early as 8:00 a.m., and I've seen tournament games start as early as 7:00 a.m. (to allow for up to two additional games in the same day). Unless you are willing to drag your child out of bed at a completely uncivilized hour to eat his precompetition meal (which seems like a bit of overkill to me), you'll probably need to feed him a little differently for early games. Have a good healthy dinner the night before, just like you normally would. Even if you have a policy against post-dinner snacks, consider giving your child some-thing to top off her tank just before bed. Good choices might include crackers and cheese or an apple. In the morning, keep the breakfast light. You don't want to weigh her down with anything heavy or difficult to digest. When I was a player, I always found that a small bowl of oatmeal and half a container of yogurt was about the right combination for me. My kids also like fruit smoothies—I always sneak in protein—and scrambled eggs before a game. Experiment until you find the combination that works best for your child. Just remember—keep it small, keep it relatively high-carb, and keep it easy to digest.

healthy food and don't hinder or replace meals.

* If eating healthier is a battleground in your house like it is in mine, modeling healthy eating helps. It also helps to provide convenient access to healthy alternatives. I think when kids grab bad choices, it is often because they're very hungry, and the bad choices happen to be the most handy. Provide equally convenient healthy choices, and reduce the number of bad choices available. If the junk isn't in the house, chances are they won't eat so much of it.

* For specific ideas and guidelines, be sure to check out the USDA's current food pyramid (http://mypyramid.gov). It isn't what you remember as a child.

Game Snacks: A Team Thing or on Your Own?

At the risk of irritating all of Florida's orange growers, I have to say that I am not a big fan of the ubiquitous team half-time snack. I don't know about you, but I have enough to worry about without having to keep track of when it is my turn to run out and buy oranges and other little snacks for the entire team. Nor do I necessarily want my kids given sugary fruit snacks, cupcakes, or other common team snacks during or immediately after a game. I would much rather provide just the right nutrition for my own child, in a form that I know he will happily eat. If that's not enough of a reason, consider too that in this age of ever-increasing food allergies, the team snack idea could be downright dangerous in some cases.

GAME DAY

You will, of course, want your child to eat soundly all the time. Still, for the best performance, there are a few additional pointers to keep in mind on game days.

Pre-game: Timing matters. If the time allows, have your child eat approximately two hours before game time. Any later, and part of the body's energy will be dedicated to digestion. Help her choose a relatively light mix of carbohydrates and lean protein, such as a turkey sandwich. Including some fats in the meal is just fine, but don't make them the main player, because they can slow digestion. Don't let her skip a meal either. The body needs replenished glycogen stores in order to function optimally.

Post-game recovery: Getting some nutrients back into the body after game time helps build the body back up for the next event. To accomplish this, it is a really good idea to have a healthy high carbohydrate snack available immediately after the game. A piece of fruit and plenty of water are ideal. Your child should follow this with a balanced meal within another two hours or so to continue recovery.

Slow cookers: making post-practice dinners possible across the country

Remember the ever-present Crock Pots® your mother used in the '60s and '70s? They're back and in a big way. I'm not quite sure why they ever fell out of favor, because they are brilliant and have saved many a frantic soccer family from yet another fast-food meal. The idea is simple: Throw together the ingredients for dinner when you have time—say in the morning, or the evening before—then simply plug in the slow cooker in the morning and forget about it. The meal will be ready when you get back from all of your running around. Even better, if you live in a multi-player household, the meal will be ready and hot for everyone, whenever they get home. It is an easy matter to modify your favorite recipes for use in a slow cooker, but there are many great cook books out there.

Sports drinks and bars: Don't go overboard on specialty sports drinks and bars. Nutrients are nutrients, and they don't get improved by being compressed into bars. In fact, in many cases the nutrients are actually less effective in these artificial forms. Natural whole foods are your best bet. For example, the University of Washington's athletic department has been using chocolate milk as a recovery drink for several years now. Think about it: it is a great combination of carbohydrates and protein that is also pleasant for most athletes to drink. If you want to use sports bars and drinks for convenience, fine, but don't do it because you think the nutrition is better.

HYDRATION

The topic of hydration isn't exactly glamorous, but it is incredibly important, even more so for young athletes than adults. Inadequate hydration not only leads to poor performance, but it can also be very dangerous, especially on hot days.

Make sure your child knows that by the time he is thirsty, it

Know the Signs of Dehydration

Dehydration during sports is much more common than you might think, and thirst is not an accurate gauge. To help protect your child, it is a great idea to watch for these signs of dehydration:

* Unexpected fatigue   * Nausea   * Dark urine
* Headache   * Weakness   * Irritability
* Dizziness   * Muscle cramping * Confusion

is already too late. Don't let him make the mistake of drinking only during a game. According to the U.S. Soccer Federation and the American Academy of Pediatrics, he should prep the body by drinking 8 to 16 ounces in the hour or so leading up to the game. During the game, he should take in additional fluids every 20 minutes: 5 ounces per 20 minutes for kids weighing less than 90 lbs., and 9 ounces per 20 minutes for kids weighing 90 lbs. or over. And finally, he should drink at least 16 ounces after a game.

How can you be sure your child is getting the correct amount of fluids before a game? Try weighing him both before and after the game. If he has lost weight, it means that he has not adequately replaced the fluids lost during the activity. If he has gained weight, he may have taken in too many fluids.

As with nutrition, moderation matters. In most cases, drinking plain water is just fine. However, drinking plain water in extreme amounts can lead to hypernutremia, which is essentially a condition of over hydration. When an athlete drinks plain water in excessive amounts, it can dilute the body's electrolyte balance. If it is so hot that your player must drink extensively, consider providing a sports drink containing electrolytes. Another alternative to consider: there are now electrolyte tablets on the market that can be kept in a tube in the sports bag and then added to any bottle of water. Finally, be careful of caffeine because it is a diuretic.

TYPES OF SURFACES

Why should you care what kind of surface your child is playing on? Because each surface plays so differently, each one ideally also requires a different kind of cleat. You can also expect that the surface will affect the way that the game is played and even the likelihood of injury.

There are as many field surfaces as there are soccer fields. Each one has its own unique feel and playing characteristics. Still, it is convenient to think of field surfaces as grouped into several common categories.

NATURAL GRASS

In most parts of the country, the vast majority of the fields you will come across are covered in natural grass. High-quality natural turf is the surface of choice throughout the world. *High-quality* is the operative phrase here. A high-quality artificial turf field will be much preferred over a low-quality natural surface. The playing characteristics of natural grass fields vary a great deal. The ideal surface will be uniform and soft enough to provide some *give,* allowing the player's cleats to sink in slightly, but not so much that it slows down the progress of the ball. The ideal cleat choice for this type of surface will depend entirely on the characteristics of the field on game day. A firm ground cleat is most common, but very hard fields will require hard-ground cleats or turf shoes while soft fields will require—you guessed it—soft-ground cleats.

FIELD TURF

While natural grass may be the surface of choice, it isn't always economical, environmentally sound, or even feasible in extreme cases. Regular and persistent droughts in parts of the western states means that grass cannot be grown there without serious irrigation. Heavy rains in other parts of the country lead to muddy, mucky fields, unless the field has been installed with an expensive professional drainage system. Increasingly, more communities are turning to the consistent and trouble-free playing characteristics offered by FieldTurf®. Unlike the old indoor-outdoor carpet-looking turf of old, FieldTurf® looks, feels, and plays just like high-quality natural grass. The secret lies in a base layer composed of tiny rubber particles that simulate soil. You'll know when your child is playing on FieldTurf® surfaces because you will find these tiny particles EVERYWHERE. That minor inconvenience aside, players love FieldTurf®. It doesn't get hard or muddy, yet it has enough give that it provides a very comfortable playing surface. Firm-ground cleats are perfect in this case.

Is turf safe?

The answer to this question depends in large part upon the type of artificial turf we're talking about. Modern FieldTurf® surfaces simulate natural grass so well that they don't cause any more injuries or difficulty than the natural surface would. The old style Astro®turf was known to cause turf burns (which are rather like carpet burns). Because it is so hard, slipping was common, which led in turn to related injuries such as twisted ankles and knees. My teammates and I found shin splints more common during indoor season, when we were playing on the hard, unforgiving surface.

Clay or Other Non-grass Surfaces

In some parts of the world, particularly South America, there is no grass involved at all. These hard surface fields usually are made of clay or compacted dirt. While relatively rare in the U.S., I have come across this type of field from time to time. Obviously a hard-surface field calls for hard ground cleats or turf shoes.

Indoor soccer surfaces

By virtue of being inside and away from sun and rain, artificial surfaces are the only option for an indoor arena. The best indoor arenas use FieldTurf®-style surfaces. Your player can choose between firm-ground, turf shoes or indoor shoes. A few older arenas use old-style Astro®turf. These surfaces are very hard and have an indoor/outdoor carpet feel to them. Only turf shoes or indoor shoes should be used.

8 Keeping it Real: Tips for Healthy Families

Throughout this book, we've discussed many objective elements of the game of soccer. We've talked about the rules, the lines on the field, and the required equipment—all very black and white topics. That's the easy part.

The trickiest aspects of soccer parenting, however, have nothing to do with the facts. The hard part is related to all of those gray areas, such as how to best support your child, when to let her quit, or how to navigate the complexities of a multi-family household. Each family has to find its own solutions to these problems, so I can't tell you exactly what you should do. What I can do is offer tips and points for your consideration based upon my own hard-won experience and upon the experi-

ence of the many other Soccer Moms I've spoken to. I hope that you'll take what is offered in this section and twist and shape it to make it your own. Put it into whatever form works best for your family and your needs.

This section is all about soccer parenting, so we'll start with a discussion of the benefits of the role and how to play it to its best effect in *The Benefits of Soccer Parenting*. Even the best sports parent can't protect her children from every problem. In *Helping Your Player Through the Rough Spots*, we'll tackle a few of the most common sticky situations such as player burn-out. Because families come in all shapes and sizes, *Special Family Situations* shares tips for multiple-household families and single moms. As different as our families all are, one thing that I'm sure we all have in common is the need for more time; *Making the Most of Your Time* will help you do just that.

THE BENEFITS OF SOCCER PARENTING

Way back at the beginning of the book, we spent a lot of time talking about all of the benefits to your child of participating in soccer. But what about you?

There ought to be an upside for you to justify all of the hours, effort, and dollars you'll expend during your soccer parenting years. Here are just a few of my personal favorites, though of course your mileage may vary:

* It is fun for me too! Soccer has become a central part of our family's social life. Every time we go to a soccer game, we not only get to watch our kids having fun, getting great exercise, and learning valuable lessons, but we also get to hang out with good friends on the sidelines.

* All that time driving back and forth provides lots of quality time with my boys.

* It provides a relief from some of the usual teenage worries—every moment they are playing soccer, I can be reasonably sure they aren't getting into any trouble!

* Soccer provides lots of opportunities for great conversations with my boys. Even though it is just a game, it provides a useful framework for talking about a lot of other important life lessons.

YOUR ROLE AS A SPORTS PARENT

Everyone will have their own opinion on this topic, of course, but if you ask me, I'd say that your job as a sports parent is to provide the love, support, encouragement, wisdom and guidance that will allow your child to most fully enjoy the game. Sure, there are logistical roles to fill too; you also get the job of paying the fees and arranging transportation, but I think it is in the softer areas that our kids need us the most.

It is probably just as important to discuss what your job is *not*. Unless you also happen to be the coach, your job is not to help your child learn specific skills or become a better player. You can help by providing training space and tools at home, but it is best to leave the primary responsibility for soccer skill-building to the coach. Similarly, it is not your job to solve on-field problems or to dissect and improve the team's strategy. Your child has a coach for all of that. What they need you to be is a parent.

Now, a lot of that is much easier said than done, especially if you happen to know a little something about the game. In that case, there probably isn't any harm in discussing soccer with your kids, when *they* want to and if *they* bring it up. Do try to give them time to decompress after a game before you let the conversation turn back to soccer.

How do I know if my child played well or poorly?

The reality is that, unless you are knowledgeable about soccer's finer points, you may not necessarily know whether she's played well or not. You can see what she is doing on the field, and you can tell whether she is hustling and demonstrating skill. What you can't necessarily tell is whether she is doing what the coach has asked her to do or whether she is playing properly within the team's strategy. But that's OK, because it isn't your job to judge her anyway. Your job is to support her, encourage her, and cheer her on.

And by all means, try to make sure that soccer doesn't become all that you talk about with your child. This too can be harder than it sounds when you've got a player who eats, sleeps, and breathes soccer. As difficult as it is, I think it is worth the effort to be conscious of talking about non-soccer related topics as often as you can.

BEING A POSITIVE FAN

As a supportive parent, you'll probably be watching a lot of games. The more you learn and the longer you watch, the more you'll get into the excitement. Just be sure that when you are cheering your child on from the sidelines that you are doing so in a positive manner. In the heat of the game, many players don't hear the words you are saying, but they most definitely hear the tone. Make sure it is a positive one and remember how easy it can be to embarrass a child.

Enthusiasm is great, but there are times when it can go too far. One team I know had a number of very loyal fans, most of whom were really appreciated at each game. One fan, however, eventually got to be a little too loyal and would spend the entire game yelling at the referee, the opposing players, or even the coach. This was grating to all of the players, but was just plain no fun for his two daughters on the team. It eventually got to the point where they asked him not to come to important games, because of the extra stress he caused them.

How to recognize if you've gone too far? If your voice is hoarse after a game, you've probably been saying too much, especially if it wasn't all positive. If your child starts to indicate in any way that she'd rather you not come watch games, or seems at all stressed-out by your presence, there is probably a reason. That should be a clue to take a good look at your behavior.

If you do get any signs that you are over-involved, take a step back and remind yourself that it is just a game, that you

M😊m Tip
How to Chill

Having a tough time relaxing and remaining positive at the game? Try listening to relaxing music. It is a bizarre, but interesting, experience. The game takes on almost the character of a dance. The kind of music dictates the kind of experience. It is hard to get too worked up with something like Debussy's Reverie playing. If that doesn't work, another parent I know used to suck on lollipops to help keep quiet.

can't relive your sports days vicariously through your child, and that you should just let her play. Try to consciously take on a relaxed and positive position by doing things like applauding a good play from either team, demonstrating good sportsmanship, and giving the referee and coaches the benefit of the doubt.

Above all, please try not to criticize your child. If his play needs some improvement or correction, let the coach do it. There is really nothing to be gained if you jump in, especially in a public setting. You'll only embarrass your child and probably won't correct the behavior anyway. Ask yourself why you feel it necessary to be critical, and then give yourself a solid reality check—your child almost certainly isn't headed to the professional ranks anyway, so why push him hard now? I know it is easier said than done, but your goal should be to sit back, relax, and enjoy watching the game unfold.

SUPPORTING AND REWARDING GOOD SPORTSMANSHIP

It should go without saying, but good sportsmanship in kids starts with positive modeling from the adults in their lives. Unfortunately, too many parents will behave poorly on the sidelines, then wonder how their kids turn out to be poor sports. Deep down, I think we all know these things already, but sometimes it helps to have a reminder;

* Teach your child to win graciously. If the team wins, don't allow your child to make any derisive comments about the other team, even in private.

* Teach him how to lose graciously too: If the team has lost, please don't go in for the negative remarks, like blaming it on the referee or saying that the other team didn't deserve to win.

* Do your best not to yell at the referee, coaches or players.

* The mechanics of good sportsmanship really matter. Little niceties like shaking hands after the match are important and should be followed no matter what.

* Don't allow any trash talking, humiliating comments or taunting and certainly don't engage in them yourself. Yes, you'll probably be tempted on occasion, but repeat after me... "It's a game and these are kids... It's a game and these are kids..."

* Teach your kid the wisdom of walking away if necessary. The ugly reality is that some teams are actually taught how to take cheap shots when the referee isn't looking. It will happen, but that doesn't mean that you or your child has to sink to that level.

* Get in the habit of complimenting good play when you see it, both in your child's teammates, and in the other team. Get them to think in terms of appreciating quality play from any source.

HELPING YOUR PLAYER THROUGH ROUGH SPOTS

Even the most positive soccer parent around may find that her child encounters a few difficult situations along with way. We'll discuss just a few of the most common situations here, along with suggestions for how to handle them gracefully.

BURNOUT

With kids at the competitive levels of soccer now playing year round or close to it, it isn't surprising that burnout is such a common problem—both for the kids and for the parents. Recognizing the signs of burnout can be tricky, but the solution is obvious; scale the participation back down to a manageable level.

I've experienced burnout both as a player and as a parent. Many of the signs are pretty common sense. You should suspect burnout if you start to see the following in your child:

* Irritability or other personality changes

* Making up excuses to avoid practice or games, such as faking an injury or pretending to be sick

* Inconsistent or declining performance in the game

* Sudden changes in eating or sleeping patterns

* Starting to put too much pressure on himself, as evidenced by emotional stress

✱ Physical signs of overtraining

My own burnout came when I was 14 years old. I loved the sport and had been playing non-stop since I was 6 years old. By the time I was 14, the level of competition had picked up substantially, and I was starting to feel the pressure. As an early teenager at the end of middle school, I was also starting to feel the pull of a social life. The combination of the two made me doubt whether I wanted to continue playing at a competitive level, which took up so much time. I just wasn't having fun anymore, but I really knew there was a problem when I found myself looking for excuses to avoid going to practices.

It seemed to me like a big decision at the time, and I remember worrying that I'd let down my teammates, coach, and family if I took time off. Of course none of that turned out to be true, and looking back, I should have known that my family in particular would be completely supportive if I took a step back. In the end, I remember going tearfully to my mom to admit that I didn't want to play the next season. She didn't miss a beat. She reminded me that this was supposed to be fun, and that if it wasn't anymore, there wasn't any point in playing. Her calm and reassuring attitude gave me the perspective to see that taking a break really was a reasonable option.

So, that's what I did. I took a season completely off. I got the break I needed and I got a chance to see that I'd been playing soccer so much for a reason. I had a chance to try out a few other activities, which clearly confirmed for me that I was most definitely better suited as a soccer player than as a cheerleader!

I really believe that had I not had a chance to take that break, or had someone else pushed me to play, I would have started to see the game as a chore and something to resent. Instead, I returned to my team the very next year a happier player. In fact, I think I was a better player for my renewed passion.

If your player comes to you with any signs of burnout and asks to take a break, I hope that you'll take the approach that my mom did; let her know that it is perfectly OK. Keep in mind, too, that your player may indeed be burned out, but be insecure about coming forward. If you see the signs, by all means bring it up and let your player know that taking a break is a feasible option.

Lest you be afraid that your child's break will cause her to get behind and not be able to catch up later, let me just say that I've since seen the same situation happen a number of times now. Not everyone does come back after a break. But among those who did come back, I didn't see a single one of them suffer or get behind. It always worked out just fine.

To Quit or Not to Quit

At some point in your sports parenting career, you may face a situation where your child wants to quit—at least temporarily— whether because of burnout or any number of other factors. The age-old question, of course, is whether you should let him. On the one hand, you want to teach him to follow through on what he starts and to know the satisfaction of successfully working through challenging situations. On the other hand, you don't want him to stay in an unhealthy, unhappy situation, particularly when there is no reasonable solution in sight. Remember, these are games we're talking about, and if they're no longer fun, we have to then question the value of continuing.

In the end, there is no simple prescription for this situation. To the question of whether it's OK to let your child quit, I can only say "maybe." What I can definitely suggest, however, is that you make sure your child knows he is always welcome to have the discussion with you. With the lines of communication open, you will be able to help her name and identify the source of frustration. Often, with your guidance, she will be able to work through the problem and will no longer want to quit. Sometimes all she needs is the chance to vent her frustration to a sympathetic listener

who can provide some needed perspective.

If, after an open and honest conversation with you, she is still determined to quit, you'll probably want to have a look at the reasons why and act accordingly. If you think that she is only frustrated by a temporary difficulty in picking up a challenging skill, or is unhappy about the amount of playing time, both of which are situations likely to pass with time, a waiting period might be all she needs. Teenagers are infamous for needing the occasional "cooling-off" period after a disagreement with the coach or another player. Suggesting that she try some new strategies for another few weeks before a final decision is made shows her that you understand her concerns and helps her feel that she does have some control in the situation. It also buys some time for temporary frustrations to pass.

If the situation is something more significant and is unlikely to improve on its own over a short period of time, quitting may indeed be the most healthy option. At this point, you'll need to consider the timing. If it is between seasons, by all means, let her take a break. The break I took when I was 14 was exactly what I needed. If the difficulty occurs near the early part of the season, there is probably little harm in stepping aside. By the same token, if the problem arises near the end of the season, you'll probably want to encourage your child to stick it out and finish up the season. Doing so allows your child to get some closure and is easier on her teammates.

One Soccer Mom told me that her mother had a clear policy about quitting that she is grateful for to this day. She and her siblings had one month to try any activity on for size. If they didn't like it for any reason, they could quit with no questions asked in that first month. Once the month was up, if they chose to continue, they had to see the activity through to the end of the season or the end of the year, whichever came first. I think this is a policy that makes sense. It gives the child the freedom to try out new things, with an escape hatch for activities that turn out to be a bad fit. Yet it also teaches the value of sticking with the activities that you've chosen to commit to.

With all that said, there are some problems that warrant quitting even mid-season. These will usually be serious enough that you'll know one when you see it. For example, if your player is so severely burned out or is otherwise feeling such intense pressure that his health and well-being are threatened, he should be allowed to quit immediately. The same goes for some chronic injuries that may become recurrent if not rested, or if your child is being in any way mistreated.

In any case, let me leave you with this thought; if your child is talking about quitting, it means he isn't having any fun, and that's a problem worth your attention.

MAKE THE DECISION TO CHANGE TEAMS

If your child loves the sport, but is simply not a good match with his existing team, whether because of the coach or other players, you may need to think about changing teams. Changing between seasons is a simple thing and is hardly even worth discussing. Like quitting, however, the question of changing teams mid-season is much trickier.

In all of my years as a Soccer Mom, this situation has only come up once. When one of my sons was about 14, the situation on his existing team had become increasingly untenable as the season progressed, through no fault of his own. We discussed it often as a family, and he made many good efforts to fix the problem himself. Despite his best efforts, he got nowhere. Only after he'd exhausted all of his solo options did we step in to help, but we were also unsuccessful in getting a satisfactory resolution.

Just as we were wondering what our next step should be, he was offered a position on another team that was an excellent fit. This was mid-season, mind you, and outside of the issue at hand, he really liked his original teammates. Leaving the team would solve his problems and was an exciting opportunity for other reasons, but it also meant leaving his good friends in less than ideal circumstances.

I won't bore you with all of the gory details or describe the factors that went into our decision, other than to say that we really struggled with it. In the end, we decided as a family to make the change, and it turned out to be a good choice. My son had a great run with the other team for about a year and half. During that interval, the league board resolved the issue he'd been having with his original team. At the start of the next season, he went back to his original team, where's he's happily been ever since.

One thing that helped the transition between teams is that he tried to handle the situation respectfully, both out of consideration for his teammates as well as to avoid burning bridges. Though it was a difficult conversation for a 14 year old, he notified the coach of his first team as soon as he'd made the final decision to leave. He told him about his plans, explained his reasons, and arranged to time the transition so as to minimize the disruption to the original team. He also tried to keep a positive tone when he told his teammates.

Even with all of this careful handling, there was a small, but vocal minority who were angry with his decision and felt that the team had been betrayed. I remember one of our friends on the team advising me not to worry about it too much because he'd always found that people can get over almost anything in three or four months. Sure enough, that's exactly what happened. Thanks in part to the bridges that he avoided burning when he first left the team, there is no trace (visible, anyway) of any remaining hard feelings.

Though it wasn't any fun at the time, I think that the whole experience taught my son a lot about dealing with sticky situations, how to self-advocate, and that he has the power to create positive change for himself. I really believe that had he stayed where he was during that pivotal year, he likely would have quit soccer altogether.

SPECIAL FAMILY SITUATIONS

Today's families come in all shapes and sizes. If your child divides his time between multiple households or if you are a single Soccer Mom (or both!), you'll have a few extra things to think about, but you certainly aren't alone. These tips might make your job just a little bit easier.

Co-Parenting a Soccer Family with an Ex-Spouse

If you and your ex-spouse can get along well enough to both go to games and cheer side by side, that's great. You may no longer be married to your ex-spouse, but you are both still the parents of your children, and they deserve to have both of your support. It is very healthy for your children to see that you can set your differences aside when it comes to supporting them.

If you can't manage to be civil, it is better to divide up the games. I'll never forget the very public knock-down-drag-out argument that my friend's recently divorced parents had at a game when I was about 12. It was embarrassing for everyone there. If it is still a vivid memory for me many years later, can you imagine what it must be like for my poor friend? Please, do whatever it takes to avoid creating these kinds of negative memories for your kids, even if it means that you don't get to go to all of the games.

If you feel you need to go the route of dividing up the games, please don't ever, ever ask your child which parent they'd like

The family calendar in the sky

The online calendar may be the best invention for busy families since the mini-van. It is especially useful for multi-household families. There are a number of good, free services out there. We've used online calendars from Google, Yahoo, AirSet, and Zoho. Our current calendar of choice is the Google calendar, but any of these choices will work just fine. The idea is to create a centralized family calendar that can be accessed by either parent at any time. You can even set up the calendar to automatically create email or text reminders about important events.

to see at which game. That is an impossible decision for a child to make, so as parents, you should make that decision for her. Divide up the games in any manner that works for you and your ex-spouse, just don't ask your child to weigh in on the decision.

If you and your ex-spouse share custody, consider working out the living schedule so that sports and other extra-curricular activities can be accommodated. Ask any divorce expert, and they'll tell you that providing normalcy and consistency for your kids is one of the best things that you can do to get them through the difficult divorce transition.

Try to do a good job of coordinating the communication between spouses so that the coach or team manager don't have to do it for you. Have a plan up front to make sure nothing falls through the cracks. Despite your best efforts, a few things still will. It is very easy for each parent to think that the other parent has paid a fee or turned in a form. Getting in the habit of copying each other on team email discussions can really help.

Some families find that regular phone calls help them keep on track. But even if you don't want to have to talk frequently with your ex-spouse, there are still ways to communicate effectively. A shared online family calendar, for example, is an excellent tool for keeping everyone on track. In fact, this is a tool that *all* families, divorced or not, can take advantage of.

If your kids split their time between two households, I can pretty much guarantee you that managing equipment will become a major issue. To minimize last-minute runs to pick up a forgotten shinguard or jersey, it is extremely useful to maintain a dedicated gear bag (see the *Store it in the Bag* sidebar). In theory, with all gear returned to the gear bag immediately after use or washing, it is only a matter of grabbing the bag when it is time to run to the other house. It can also be helpful to keep an extra set of socks and shinguards at each house.

Make the choice together about what level of soccer involvement is appropriate. Even if one parent has primary custody, chances are that you'll both be paying for the activity, and you'll both be doing at least some of the driving. It is only fair that you're in on the decisions together. To short-circuit future disagreements, when you have the discussion about whether or not to sign up for a particular league or activity, why not work out the details around schedules, transportation, money, and so on at that time?

Even after you've all fully committed to signing up for the team, the need for family decision making doesn't stop there. Continue to make family decisions together. When one of our sons wanted to switch to another team, we all met for coffee to discuss the situation and made the decision together.

Surviving Soccer Season as a Single Mom

One of my very favorite Soccer Moms is also a single parent. When I asked her for her advice to other single sports parents, her (only slightly) tongue-in-cheek response was "Don't do it."

But she does do it, because her kids love it so much. If you catch her on one of her less hectic days, she'll tell you that she's

SOCCER SIBLINGS

At multi-field complexes there will be a lot of people at any given time. It is very easy for kids to slip away while you are caught up in the action of the game, or to become confused about which field to return to.

* Make sure that your family has a *what-to-do-if-I-get-lost plan* in action. Agree on a family meeting place at each field. Many complexes have a concession stand that is visible even from a child's perspective at a distance.

* Remind young children about the usual rules of caution with strangers. Fields are public areas, and the same common sense applies here. Above all, make sure they know they have permission to make a scene if necessary to get help.

* Accompany young children to the restroom.

glad she does too. So *how* does she do it?

First, and foremost, she asks for help when she needs it. For the most part, it is transportation help that she needs, because she can't be in more than one place at a time. With multiple kids playing sports and a demanding full-time job, she knows that she has to make sure to set up at least one solid carpool partnership on each child's team.

She's also necessarily very organized. She plans ahead to figure out which child she'll drive to practice and which child she'll have to send with a teammate. To keep all three kids fed on their hectic schedule the organization and planning has to extend to meal times too. It might be that they don't all manage to eat together every weekday, and it might be that there's some fast food thrown in from time to time, but that's OK; she knows that she has to choose her battles.

She has made it clear to her kids that she'd like to be at all of their events, but simply has to make some hard choices from time to time. They understand that, and are always happy to give play-by-play commentary after each game. She also invites them to speak up when any game or event is particularly important. In some cases, she's even been known to send a video camera along to games that she must miss. In any case, she tries hard (usually successfully) to avoid the guilt trap. She knows that the decisions she makes have to work for the entire family.

MAKING THE MOST OF YOUR TIME

You might be an expert juggler of multiple players and multiple commitments, but you can only be in one place at a time. Here are some ways to make the most of the time during soccer season.

CARPOOLING STRATEGIES

Carpooling is, of course, the answer to the maintenance of everyone's sanity. Here are a few tips for creating and managing a carpool that keeps everyone happy.

Actively seek out carpooling partners at the beginning of the season, before you need them, because you almost certainly will. Be sure to work out the details early on too. Avoiding miscommunication and hassle is well worth a few minutes of extra organizing up front. You might want to think about how to answer questions like: Who will drive and when? Where will you pick up? How long will you wait if someone isn't ready? Are there any rules, like no eating in the car?

Get everyone's information. One of my son's teams makes up a laminated card each year with the entire team's cell phone numbers. If you don't have that, at least make up a sheet with the contact info for all carpool participants.

Carry emergency medical information. This might sound paranoid, but it really is a good idea to have this information in case anything happens while other players are in your care. Also, have a back up plan. What if the scheduled driver has come down with the flu?

Be sure to take your turn whenever you possibly can. A carpool is just bumming a ride if you always make the other parties drive. Besides, you might very well enjoy getting to know the other team players during the ride.

WHAT TO DO WHILE YOU'RE WAITING

If your child plays soccer for very long, you will surely find yourself with a lot of time to fill. You will be waiting during practices, during game warm ups, and between games at away tournaments. That can add up to a lot of time.

Depending upon how close you live, you may be able to drop them off, go home, and then return for a pickup. But why waste all of the gas and time spent driving back and forth? With a little bit of pre-planning, you can use soccer practice time in many productive ways. You can even learn to be grateful for the little bit of personal time it can give you.

To take best advantage of the waiting time, you'll need to think ahead just a little bit. As tasks come up in your day-to-day life, keep note of which of those could be accomplished during your soccer wait times. Before you head out to a practice or game, simply scan your list to choose the candidates for that day, and grab any necessary materials. I highly recommend that you read productivity guru David Allen's *Getting Things Done* for a simple-to-manage and highly effective personal productivity system that is very Soccer Mom friendly.

Here are just a few ideas for productive or fun ways to spend your many waiting hours.

* Write a book! (And just to prove my point, I am writing this very section from my car during my youngest son's soccer practice). If not a book, how about a blog, or a journal, or even a few thank-you notes?

* Read a good book—either by yourself, or read out loud if you have other children along for the ride.

* Get some exercise! Meet another mom for a walk around the fields, go for a jog, or stick your bike in the car and go for a ride.

* Listen for relaxation, learning, or fun. A portable MP3 player can be the Soccer Mom's best friend. Download a new album you've never heard before and listen to it in peace and quiet; learn a foreign language using audio programs like Pimsleur®, or download podcasts related to your favorite hobby or interest.

* Meditate.

* Work on hand crafts to both relax and bring out your inner creativity. Knitting and hand quilting are both very portable and lend themselves well to this application.

* Catch up on your phone calls.

* Keep a file of office paperwork handy and ready to go on short notice for waiting times.

* Practice your sports photography skills.

* Grab some cookbooks from home, and plan your menus for the week.

* Watch a movie on a portable DVD player.

* Arrange to meet with the other moms to catch up on the latest

gossip.

* Sit back and enjoy watching your child laugh, play, and be active.

* Catch up on your email, sort out your calendar, or do other productivity-related tasks.

9 Taking It to the Next Level

If your child really, truly has a passion for the game, your family may one day end up having to make a decision about whether he should take it up a notch and pursue **elite level play.** When the time comes to make the decision, chances are that it won't be as difficult to make as you might think. Both you and your child will probably have a pretty good idea by that time about whether your child has what it takes, and whether your family situation will allow the ramped-up commitment and cost.

The purpose of this section is to give you the information you need in order to make an informed decision. Picking up where we left off from the League Structure discussion in Sec-

tion 2, we'll cover the levels of play that are available for players who are ready to move beyond the select and travel teams.

If your child isn't yet at this age, keep in mind that participation at these levels and beyond is relatively rare. To keep up at the levels described in this section requires a serious dedication to the sport, near year-round participation, and substantial family resources (both in terms of time and effort). All of these factors together preclude meaningful participation in other activities. There are indeed kids for whom elite-level participation does make sense, but it is best to go in with your eyes open.

In this section, we'll start with a quick comparison of the elite team options so that you can get a feel for the relative time and money commitments of each before we move on to discussing them in detail. We'll then take a closer look at the age-group development options, including the U.S. Soccer Development Academy and Olympic Development Programs. Finally, we'll discuss opportunities for playing at a collegiate level.

COMPARING ELITE TEAM OPTIONS

Once your child reaches the highest levels of the sport, the cost and time commitments go up dramatically. Before we talk about each of the options in more detail, here's a quick summary of what you can expect.

The costs provided here include league fees, equipment, tournament fees, coaching fees, and travel expenses. Because the amount of travel required varies widely by region, it is impossible to give exact financial and time commitments. Instead, please regard them as rough estimates and use them as relative comparisons to other team options.

Olympic Development Program (ODP)

Typical Season Calendar: ODP has no regular season. This is supplemental for elite players, consisting of monthly training and regional tournaments. For the very top players, this program has largely been supplanted by the U.S. Soccer Development Academy, which provides ODP-like experiences year round.

Games: Roughly one weekend per month during the playing season, plus special tournaments.

Travel: The amount of travel depends upon how far the player lives from ODP program site for their state. Periodic out-of-state tournaments are common.

Cost: <$1,500-$2,000. Note that this cost is in addition to select club team costs.

Elite U16-U19 (U.S. Soccer Development Academy)

Typical Season Calendar: One season that runs September to June, with playoffs in July. Short breaks over Christmas and Easter. Academy team players may not participate on any other team during season, with the exception of high school or national team duties—in theory. In practice, time commitments and team policies preclude high school participation for most.

In-Season Weekly Commitment: Three to four practices per week, lasting 90–120 minutes each.

Games: 30–38 games per season, each lasting 80–90 minutes, roughly once per week. Several games may be consolidated in a day or weekend on occasion to accommodate long travel distances (i.e., a team traveling from another state may play two games in the same weekend, rather than travel twice).

Travel: Extensive inter-state and international travel; regular league games are played against academy teams in other states. Families can expect at least one plane trip per month during the season.

Cost: $2,500-$5,000. Extensive travel is mostly subsidized.

U.S. Soccer U17 Men's Residency Program

Typical Season Calendar: This program follows the academic calendar. Players are chosen on a semester-by-semester basis.

In-Season Weekly Commitment: Players live on campus full-time with daily training sessions.

Travel: Extensive international travel and frequent world-class competition.

Cost: Fully funded by the U.S. Soccer Federation.

College

Typical Season Calendar: August through November.

In-Season Weekly Commitment: Practices on every school day without a game, lasting two-plus hours each. Additional fitness and weight training.

Games: Approximately two games per week, each lasting 80–90 minutes.

Travel: Extensive.

Cost: <$200 (Usually limited to the cost of cleats and shinguards, unless you count tuition.)

AGE-GROUP DEVELOPMENT PROGRAMS

When it is time to move beyond even the select and travel team levels, the primary choices are the Olympic Development Program, the US Soccer Development Academy and the U.S. Soccer Residency Program.

We'll look at an overview of each of these programs so that you'll know what to expect if your child has the opportunity to participate **in any of them.** As soccer becomes a more significant sport at the national and professional level in the U.S., the opportunites to start young are increasing.

M🌑m Tip

Family considerations

Don't take this decision lightly, as it may very well change the direction of your player's career. Your player really does have to have both elements—the skill and the passion—to make the time and effort associated with this program worthwhile. Unless you happen to live very near your state's ODP training center, participation in the program will sign you up for a lot of driving and will consign your player to a lot of time in the car and away from friends and other social activities.

OLYMPIC DEVELOPMENT PROGRAM

Until 2007, the Olympic Development Program, commonly referred to as ODP, represented the highest level of play available for youth players in the United States. With the introduction of the U.S. Soccer Development Academy (USSDA or Academy), the ODP program no longer has quite the luster that it once did for older players. Still, for strong players who don't have access to an Academy team, the ODP program provides an excellent option for elite player development.

Here's how it works, in a nutshell. Each state maintains its own ODP program under the auspices of the U.S. Soccer Federation. State teams function as a player pool to feed regional teams, which in turn feed the National Player Pool, from which national teams are chosen. In theory, ODP scouts watch teams from all over the state play and invite all promising players to ODP tryouts.

The reality is that many deserving players don't ever get scouted. Because of the large geographic areas involved, and because the most intense competition happens in heavily populated urban centers, a really talented player from an outlying area may never be seen at all by an ODP scout. Fortunately, players can walk on to ODP tryouts. The trick is in knowing how to find the tryouts and when to look for them.

If you even *think* that your child might want to play ODP, I recommend that you visit the website for your state's soccer association which will point you to the state ODP site. It should clearly layout when your child will be eligible, as well as the local schedule for tryouts.

The ODP program is not a replacement for a player's normal club team but is instead a supplemental program. The idea is to gather the very best players in a state together from time to time to allow them to experience very high level competition under the guidance of an elite coaching staff. Players selected for the ODP program will typically visit the ODP training site one to two weekends per month for special training programs. They also will travel periodically for tournaments. Because parents bear all of the travel costs, which can be quite extensive for top players, the expense for participating in the ODP program can be quite high. Our state ODP program estimates that the cost of participating in 2009 will start at approximately $1,600. Keep in mind that this cost is in addition to the fees associated with the normal club team.

U.S. SOCCER DEVELOPMENT ACADEMY

The U.S. Soccer Development Academy, known as the Academy, was developed as an antidote to weaknesses of the current Olympic Development Program (ODP) for older elite players. Namely, that top players weren't being exposed to high level training opportunities on the continual basis necessary to develop a player pool able to compete with other countries on the world stage. Furthermore, players had to patch together their own training program by combining possibly multiple club teams, ODP, and extensive travel to tournaments. In other words, kids were getting burned out on too-frequent, lower-quality play. U.S. Soccer felt that the ticket to improving the U.S.'s development of players was to create a system that would allow top players to have consistent very high quality competition while carefully metering training to avoid burnout. Introduced in late 2007, the Academy program has been an enormous success.

Rather than start from the ground up, the U.S. Soccer Federation decided to piggyback off of the network of very strong youth programs already in existence in this country. After an exhaustive application process, U.S. Soccer has

Why Elite Players May Want to Play for the High School Team

At a recent elite club tournament I overheard the coach of one club team addressing his players and their parents after a disappointing loss. He said "We are all going to have to make a decision about whether we're going to continue to allow our players to waste three months of the year playing high school. We let them last year, and today's loss is the result." Unfortunately this is a common refrain among coaches of very high-level teams. My personal opinion, for what its worth, is that this is an unfortunate development in youth sports.

Even coaches who encourage their players to go ahead and play high school soccer will at least admonish them not to pick up any bad habits. Other coaches outright forbid their players to play high school, feeling that their skills will get rusty by playing at a lower level for a couple of months and that the presence of less skilled players will increase the chance for injury. While I have to grudgingly admit that all of that is true, I think that attitude is unfortunate and neglects to factor in some of the many benefits of participating in high school soccer.

I think that playing a varsity sport is a part of the high school experience for those lucky enough to have the opportunity. There's just something fun about representing your school and being cheered on by a

(Continued on next page.)

Why Elite Players May Want to Play for the High School Team (continued)

(Continued from previous page.)

raucous crowd of your peers. It is a chance for friends who may have been separated to reunite, and it provides a less intense, more relaxed playing atmosphere.

For those kids playing at the very highest level, it also can provide a very welcome change of pace. Take the example of one of my son's friends from a former club team. This friend was a top player even in the U.S. Soccer Development Academy, and had been named to the U18 National Team pool.

Recently, however, he came to the difficult realization that he needed to take a step back. He'd been commuting long distances to play with the top teams since he was 11 years old. At 17, he simply is worn out. But he had a really hard time taking a step off of that treadmill. He agonized over the decision because he felt that he'd be letting down all of the people who helped him get to the top. That's heavy stuff for a 17 year old. Having finally made the decision, he's looking forward to a sane schedule and to get the chance to finally play for his high school team.

I think he was brave and smart to recognize what he needed. It may even be best for his soccer career in the long run. He intends to go back to his Academy team in a few months, once he's had an opportunity to just enjoy being a teenager.

chosen 79 existing youth soccer clubs to become Academy teams. By agreeing to field Academy teams, these clubs had to adopt the format and participation guidelines laid out by U.S. Soccer. In order to expose the Academy players to the highest level of competition on a regular basis (instead of at rare special tournaments, as had been the case in the past), Academy teams from across the country were formed into regional leagues. So, where an Academy team might have previously traveled across the state for a regular league game, they might now travel several states over. During the season, many Academy team players are on airplanes at least once per month, often twice.

In return for adopting the Academy format, Academy teams are subsidized by U.S. Soccer. While it sounds rather expensive, when all is said and done, Academy teams end up being less expensive than other elite teams. As of this writing, players on Academy teams paid a fixed fee of approximately $2,500 per year. Between that fee and substantial subsidies from sponsors and U.S. Soccer, all uniforms, coaching costs, and travel are covered. In addition, the Academy offers a number of scholarships for deserving players who would be otherwise unable to play.

Perhaps the biggest difference between the ODP and Academy programs is that the Academy program is not a supplemental, occasional opportunity. It is combines the best features—from a player development standpoint—of the travel club and ODP programs. Highlights are:

* Academy clubs form two teams: U15/ U16 and U17/ U18.

* Players stay with the Academy team for an 8 month season.

* Instead of running ragged keeping track of multiple teams, as many top players had to do in the past, Academy team players may only play on the Academy team during the season. There are only two exceptions: high school and national team duties.

* Teams must train at least three days per week and have at least two days of rest per week. The remaining two days may be used for games, scrimmages, or tournaments.

* The number of games per season will be limited to 30 to 38.

While only a handful of very elite players gets to play on an Academy team, their introduction has changed the landscape for all select players. Most notably, the clubs fielding Academy teams no longer participate in normal state leagues. Perhaps even more significantly, the players on Academy teams may not participate in the ODP program. Washington state currently has two Academy teams, which in the past had been far ahead of and dominant over other elite teams in the state. Now that they are in the Academy league, the remaining teams have blossomed under the closer competition between them. Also, many more spots have opened up in the ODP program, allowing more kids to get access to that program.

Clearly, the Academy program has a lot to offer both individual players and U.S. Soccer as a whole. But it is not for everyone. It is a way of life that precludes many normal teenage activities. Many weekends for the eight-month period are occupied with travel. Also, while high school soccer play is allowed in theory, in practice very few Academy players find it actually feasible to play for their high school.

U.S. Soccer U17 Men's Residency Program

If your child is destined to be the next Landon Donovan, he may well pass through the U.S. Soccer Federation's U17 Men's Residency Program on his way to superstardom. Limited to the top 40 U17 players in the country and fully funded by the USSF, the Residency Program brings players to live and train full-time on the campus of the IMG Academy in Bradenton, Florida.

Founded in 1999, the Residency Program was designed to groom players for future U.S. Men's World Cup teams. Players are chosen on a semester-by-semester basis. While on campus, they train for several hours per day with the national team coaching staff and take accelerated high school classes. Many of the players are able to graduate a year early, making them available for college, national team, or professional play that much sooner. They are also regularly exposed to high-level international competition.

Though it has had some success, some wonder whether the role of the Residency Program will be changing in coming years. In some ways, the U.S. Soccer Development Academy program is intended to achieve many of the Residency Program's goals, but at a local level. In addition, Major League Soccer teams are now starting to field high level youth development programs of their own.

COLLEGE TEAMS

Playing in intercollegiate sports always has been an intense, pressure-filled experience. Today it is more so than it ever has been. As such, the experience isn't for everybody. Just because your child is skilled enough to play in college doesn't mean that it is right for him.

If you thought elite club play during the high school years required persistence and determination, you haven't seen anything yet. The competition on collegiate teams is tough, and the hours long. In case you do have one of those players who manages to go on to play college soccer, here's a brief primer of his options.

Division I

The very top schools in the country are in the National Collegiate Athletic Association's (NCAA) Division I, commonly referred to as DI (pronounced D-One). There currently are 342 Division I schools. These schools each have a fixed number of full scholarships to divide amongst their players. The competition for these scholarships is incredibly intense and usually involves an elaborate recruitment process that starts during a player's junior year. Participation at a Division I school is as intense as is the competition for scholarships. There is a lot of travel involved, and players have to be prepared to dedicate a great deal of time to the sport during the season. It also is common for Division I teams to redshirt freshmen. Each player normally has four years of eligibility. A player who has been redshirted can train with the team but is not eligible to play in games. In exchange, the player does not use up a year of eligibility. For teams, this practice has a lot of benefits; they are allowed to provide extra training to players before they have to use them, and it pushes up the average age of players actively competing, which for boys can be a significant advantage. For the player, however, it means that the college career lasts five years instead of four.

One last note on Division I participation. If your player goes this route, he will need to choose his school very carefully. If a player's participation on a Division I team doesn't go well, he would have to sit out a year before transferring to another Division I team. Transfers between Division II, Division III, and NAIA (National Association of Intercollegiate Athletics) teams carry no such restrictions, however. In practice, this means that many former Division I players end up transferring to Division II teams, rather than

Scholarship dreams

Lest you base any decisions about whether your child should play on an elite travel club or perhaps just a local select team on the likelihood of getting a college scholarship, let me take a moment for a little reality check. Soccer in the United States is becoming incredibly competitive. There are millions of kids playing soccer, the vast majority of whom dream of playing in college. A shockingly slim percentage (roughly 1-2%) of them actually make it. To earn a position on a college team these days requires the rare combination of extraordinary athletic talent, and a dedication to play that few kids can keep up for the years required. I've seen lots of players who seemed at age 15 or so to be a shoo-in for college play, only to burn out before they get there.

The moral of the story? Never try to justify pushing your player to play at the highest levels because of the scholarship it will bring. For the vast majority of players, even very, very good ones, it won't. If a college scholarship is your goal, good grades and strong test scores are your best bet.

wait for their waiting period to run out.

DIVISION II

The next step down is NCAA's Division II. As of this writing there were 282 Division II schools. These schools tend to be slightly smaller than Division I schools. Division II soccer is very competitive, though often more relaxed than Division I, and these teams still have a few scholarships to offer, though substantially fewer than Division I schools. However, both the competition for roster spots and the playing environment tends to be just a hair less intense than for Division I schools. Division II can be a great option for scholarship-worthy players who do not want to play Division I for whatever reason.

DIVISION III

The lowest tier of NCAA intercollegiate competition takes place in Division III. These schools have to follow slightly different rules than Divisions I and II. Notably, Division III schools cannot offer scholarships to their players. They are also not allowed to redshirt freshmen. You still have to be a strong player to get a spot on a Division III team, but you can expect

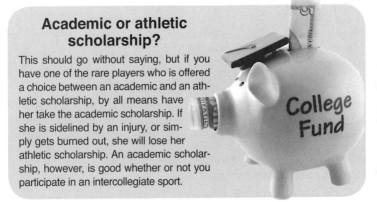

Academic or athletic scholarship?

This should go without saying, but if you have one of the rare players who is offered a choice between an academic and an athletic scholarship, by all means have her take the academic scholarship. If she is sidelined by an injury, or simply gets burned out, she will lose her athletic scholarship. An academic scholarship, however, is good whether or not you participate in an intercollegiate sport.

WHAT SHOULD MY PLAYER DO TO IMPROVE HIS RECRUITMENT CHANCES?

Any student who has dreams of playing collegiate ball has to play with the best club as early as possible. This may mean traveling long distances to train with a more competitive club. If your player lives within reach of a U.S. Soccer Development Academy team, his first step should be to try out for that. It is currently the best way to ensure both quality skill development and exposure to scouts from top-notch collegiate programs. If you don't live near an Academy team, the next best is the Olympic Development Program. Participation in elite, *college showcase*-type tournaments also helps. Players should keep their grades and test scores up; all else being equal, coaches will choose a player with a higher GPA.

Toward the end of sophomore year, your player should put together a soccer resume, which highlights his best club, high school, ODP, and Academy experiences. It should include basic academic information, such as GPA and honors or advanced placement courses taken. During the early part of his junior year, your player should start contacting the coaches of teams he is interested in via email. The email should include a resume, and information about upcoming tournaments in case the coach would like to watch. Once interested, most coaches will ask for a video. If possible, send one with an entire half of a game, rather than an edited highlight reel. Coaches want to see how your player reacts in all situations.

What are coaches looking for? Aside from technical skill, which is obvious, coaches also look for someone who is well-rounded, coachable, willing to put in the effort, and has that little something special. Truly wise coaches know that that player isn't always the best kid on the team when they are very young. In fact, being a stand-out player at age nine often has nothing to do with being a stand-out at age 17.

a more relaxed playing environment that offers a good balance between athletics and academics.

NAIA

The NAIA offers an alternative to the three divisions of the NCAA. NAIA schools tend to be smaller, private institutions. Interestingly, it is the only intercollegiate athletics association that offers international play, as NAIA has several membership schools in Canada. NAIA schools may offer scholarships, providing yet another reasonable alternative to Division I play for scholarship-worthy players. Historically, the level of competition for NAIA schools has fallen somewhere between mid-level Division II and Division III in terms of quality of play.

Resources

10 Glossary

Advantage An official rule giving the referee the latitude to ignore a foul if he feels it would benefit the team that would have otherwise had a free kick. This usually comes up when the referee thinks a good goal-scoring opportunity is imminent.

"All Ball" Said by observers when, in their opinion, a player made contact only with the ball and not with another player during a tackle. As in "C'mon ref! That was all ball!"

Assistant Referee/AR/Flagman One of two helpers to the main game official. Primary responsibilities include helping the referee to call throw-ins, goal kicks, and corner kicks, as well as indicating infractions of the offside law.

Attack The process of trying to score a goal.

Boots Another name for cleats, the special-purpose shoes worn by soccer players to improve traction and touch on the ball.

Box See Penalty Box.

Bunch Ball Affectionate name for the style of play you'll see if you watch a U6 game. There are no positions, and the whole group follows the ball around like a swarm of bees.

Captain A player who has been selected by the coach or by a vote of other team members to manage the coin toss and to serve as official team representative to the referee.

"Carry" Instruction for the player with the ball to dribble a little bit longer.

Carrying the Ball See dribbling.

Center Back/Center D Defender responsible for guarding the central portion of the field directly in front of the goal his team is defending. Depending upon the strategy the coach is using, there might be two center backs at a time.

Center Circle Located in the center of the field, and 10 yards in diameter, it comes into play only during kick-offs. When the two opposing teams line up for kick-off, the team with the kick-off will place the ball at the very center of the circle. The opposing team must remain on its own side of the midfield line, and outside of the center circle.

Chip A style of kick intended to rise up steeply and drop down over an obstacle, like the keeper or a defensive wall. This is roughly like a pitch in golf.

Cleat Studs The hard plastic nubbies found on the bottom of specialized soccer shoes. These are designed to provide traction and keep the kids on their feet and out of the mud. They'll end up in the mud anyway.

Cleats Specialized, form-fitting soccer shoes with plastic studs. They come in various styles and materials, each designed for a specific kind of field surface. You'll be buying lots of these.

Cleats Up When a player goes in for a tackle with the bottom of his shoes up and exposed. Considered a kind of cheap shot and if blatant is usually good for a yellow card.

Coin Toss The mini-ceremony before the game used to determine which team will defend which goal. Participants are the captains from both teams and the referee. The winner of the coin toss gets to choose which goal his team will defend in the first half of the game. The goals are reversed for the second half.

Corner Kick A kick awarded to the offensive team when a defending player was the last to touch a ball that went over the goal line without being a goal. The ball must be placed within one yard of the corner flag, and the opposing team has to stay at least 10 yards away.

Cross A long pass kicked to a player on the other side of the field.

Defender A player whose primary job is to keep the other team from scoring. They'll spend most of their time within the defensive third of the field.

Defense The collection of all defenders on a team, usually three or four.

Defensive Anything related to a team's attempts to prevent the opposing team from scoring.

Direct Free Kick or **Direct Kick** A special kind of kick awarded to one team when the other team has committed one of a list of specific fouls. The ball must be stationary before the kicker can take the kick. If the ball goes directly into the goal from the kick, the goal will be allowed to stand (as opposed to an indirect free kick).

Dribbling Running with the ball at the player's foot. As the player runs, he will touch the ball lightly, usually with the instep, to move it just enough forward to keep up with the running pace.

"Drop" Said usually by a player without the ball to a player with the ball to indicate that there's a player behind her that she can pass to if she wants or needs to.

Drop-Ball A method of restart used when play has been stopped due to an injury or for any other reason that cannot be attributed to either team. In theory, the referee will drop the ball between a player from each team, both of whom will try to win possession of the ball. In practice, the ball is usually conceded to the team that had possession of the ball at the time that play was stopped. It's considered bad form to do otherwise.

End Line Another name for the goal line, this is one of the two shorter lines making up the perimeter of the field.

FieldTurf® Artificial field surface that looks and plays remarkably like real grass, distinguished by lots of little rubber bits that give the field some 'give' unlike other artificial field surfaces (and that turn up later all over your house).

FIFA (Fédération Internationale de Football Association) Soccer's international sports governing body. This is the organization that establishes the international rule set for soccer and has the absolute authority for governance.

Fifty-Fifty Ball A ball that is up for grabs, or in other words, not currently in the possession of either team.

Finish Score a goal.

Finishing The act of scoring a goal.

Flagman See Assistant Referee.

Football What the rest of the world calls soccer. And it makes a lot more sense, don't you think?

Forward An offensive player whose primary responsibility is to score goals.

Foul An offense against one of soccer's rules or laws, for which some kind of free kick is awarded to the opposing team.

Free Kick A kick taken on a stationary ball to restart play after the opposing team has committed a foul. See also Direct Free Kick and Indirect Free Kick.

Friendly An informal practice soccer game, the results of which are not counted toward any league standings. Known also as a scrimmage.

From Behind When a player goes in for a tackle from behind a player. Considered dangerous play and usually results in a foul.

"Get Numbers" Instruction, usually from a coach to the members of his team, to wait for more team members to arrive before taking any definite action.

Give and Go When a player with the ball passes to another player, continues running by, and then receives the ball immediately back. Usually used as a device to get around one or more defending players.

Goal When the ball crosses the goal line between the two goal posts. Results in a point awarded to the team not defending that goal, regardless of who actually put the ball in the net. Also, the large white netted cage at either end of the field.

Goal Box A box marked on the field, measuring 6 x 20 yards on a regulation field, directly in front of each goal. The ball must be placed within the goal box for goal kicks.

Goal Kick The form of restart used when the ball has left the field of play over a goal line and an offensive player was the last one to touch it. The ball must be stationary when kicked and it must be placed on the ground within the goal box.

Goal Line One of the two shorter sides of the field's perimeter.

Goalkeeper The player responsible for guarding the net and the only player allowed to use his hands (but only within the penalty box of the goal that his team is defending).

Goal Side Anywhere in the space between an offensive player and the goal. Coaches will often say this to remind defenders to position themselves between the offensive player they are marking and the goal.

Golden Goal Special kind of overtime period that is played until either a goal is scored or the allotted overtime period has expired, whichever comes first. So called because a single goal has the power to end a game.

Half Time A short break halfway through a game's regulation playing time.

Handball A foul that occurs when a player (other than the keeper) has deliberately allowed the ball to touch his arm or hand.

Hat Trick When a single player scores three goals in the same game. Don't ask me why three is the magic number, but this is relatively rare and is considered a pretty good trick.

Heading Intentionally using the head (usually the forehead) to redirect the ball and part of the play. One of soccer's fundamental skills.

High Kick A dangerous play in which a player has kicked a ball that is high enough off the ground (usually waist level or so) to pose a danger to a nearby opposing player, according to the judgment of the referee.

Indirect Free Kick or **Indirect Kick** A special kind of kick awarded to one team when the other team has committed a foul of a particular kind. The ball must be stationary before the kicker can take the kick. The ball must touch one player in addition to the kicker before it will be allowed to stand as a goal.

Indoor Soccer A version of soccer played in an indoor arena—like hockey on grass, but without the sticks. The game is very fast and is often played in the winter between outdoor soccer seasons.

Jamboree Informal, fun tournament usually involving small-sided, short-duration games for very young players.

Juggling A soccer skill-development game in which a player tries to keep the ball continuously in the air without using his hands. MUCH harder than it looks and excellent for developing touch.

Keeper See Goalkeeper.

Kick-off The procedure used to start any period of a soccer game, as well as to restart after a goal.

Kit Another name for a player's full uniform, usually understood to consist of a color-coordinated jersey, shorts, and socks.

Late In soccer terms, used in reference to a tackle attempt that has been made after the player in possession of the ball has already played the ball. Often results in a foul.

"Man On" Phrase used to indicate to a player that an opposing player will be upon him soon, so he'd better get rid of the ball.

Marking Guarding a specific player on the other team.

Marking Backs Defenders who are guarding specific players from the other team, rather than roaming in a particular zone of the defensive area. Marking backs usually play on the outside thirds of the field.

Middie/Mid Nickname for midfielders.

Midfield The center third of the field of play.

Midfield Line A field marking that runs parallel to, and exactly halfway between, the two goal lines

Midfielder Player whose job it is to serve as the transition between the defenders and the forwards. They end up playing a little bit of both defense and offense.

"Mine" Phrase used by one player to indicate to another that he intends to win the ball, so his teammate should back off.

Nutmeg ("meg") When one player has managed to pass the ball between the legs of an opposing player. Considered embarrassing for the "megee."

Obstruction Common name for the foul that FIFA laws refer to as "impeding the progress of the player." The general idea is that a player can't throw his body in front of another player in order to slow him down, UNLESS they are both within playing distance of the ball, in which case, it is merely shielding, which is fine.

Offensive Having to do with a team's attempts to score goals. Also, the inappropriate behavior of some over-zealous fans.

Offside Position To quote the FIFA Laws, a player is in an offside position whenever "he is nearer to his opponents' goal line than both the ball and the second last opponent." Because the goalkeeper almost always is nearer the goal line than just about anyone, the second last defender generally translates to the last field playing defender.

Offside Rule One of the most commonly broken, but least understood, of the FIFA Laws. Considered broken when a player is both in an offside position and an active part of the play at the time that a ball is kicked.

Offside Trap Sneaky defensive trick, in which all defenders step forward quickly in order to catch snoozing offensive players in an offside position. But it is also a very risky trick, because if the referee doesn't see the offside call, a dangerous goal scoring opportunity can result.

"On You" Phrase intended to let a player in possession of the ball know that an opposing player is closing fast, so they'd better think about what they're going to do with the ball.

One Touch Immediately redirecting the ball to another player.

Osgood-Schlatter Disease Very common, but little recognized, cause of sore knees related to growth spurts. Most common in boys ages 13-14 and in girls ages 11-12.

Outside Backs Defensive players who play on either side of the field. Often used interchangeably with marking back, though the two terms actually mean different things.

Overlap Play in which one player makes a run from a position behind another player in order to receive a pass from that player.

Overtime Extra playing time added on to regulation game time in order to resolve a tie. Not used in all games, but is very common in tournament or play-off situations.

Own Goal When a defensive player accidentally puts the ball into the goal that her team is defending. A point will be awarded to the other team. A real bummer, but it happens.

Passing Kicking the ball from one player to another.

Penalty Box The 18 x 44 yard box (on a regulation field) that is found in front of either goal. The penalty box impacts play in two ways. First, the goalkeeper can use her hands only within the confines of this box. Second, fouls that are committed within the penalty box may result in a penalty kick.

Penalty Kick or **PK** Very dangerous goal scoring opportunity awarded whenever a player from the defending team commits a foul that would otherwise call for a direct free kick in her team's penalty area.

Pinnie Lightweight, brightly colored, sleeveless training top used during srimmage games to distinguish players on one team from another.

Pitch Another name for a soccer field.

Post Up When an attacking player receives a pass with his back to the goal (usually with his back also right up against a defender) and holds it until he can make a pass to an oncoming teammate.

Pressure Any situation in which one player is actively trying to win the ball from another.

Push Pass The most basic and accurate of all types of passes, accomplished with the inside of the foot and a deliberate follow-through. Looks rather like putting in golf, where the leg is the putter and the ball is, well, the ball.

Recreational Level of play with the lowest degree of competition and intensity. Little emphasis placed on winning, no try-outs or cuts, and all players receive lots of playing time.

Red Card A visual signal from the referee used to indicate that a player has committed a "sending-off offense." When a player receives one of these, he must leave the field immediately, and the team cannot replace him (which means they'll have to play short). He will also have to sit out the entirety of the team's next game.

Referee The game's main official, with final decision-making authority regarding the enforcement of all of the game's laws.

Restart Any one of several methods used to start play again after it has been stopped by the referee for any reason, such as for injury, a foul, or because the ball has gone out of bounds. Methods of restart include free kicks, drop ball, goal kicks, corner kicks, and throw-ins, among others.

Sackpack Soft nylon drawstring bag designed in such a way that it can be worn as a simple backpack. Commonly used by soccer players to carry the most basic training equipment to practices.

Scrimmage Practice game. See Friendly.

Select Level of competitive soccer play that requires tryouts to make a team. Competition is more intense than at the recreational level. The amount of playing time given to any one player is usually based on merit and may not be equally spread among all players.

Send Make a long or through pass to a player who is making a run onto the ball, usually behind the line of defenders.

Serve Make a pass to another player who will then have an immediate goal scoring opportunity.

Set Piece, Set Play Pre-determined play that is executed on a restart, most commonly a free kick or corner kick. Several players will have specific pre-assigned roles to play.

Sever's Disease Very common cause of heel pain in pre-adolescent children. Most common in boys ages 10-12 and in girls ages 8-10.

Shin Splints Very common source of pain and inflammation in the lower front area of a player's legs, usually the result of ramping up training intensity too quickly.

Shooting Making an attempt to score a goal.

Shut Out When the opposing team fails to score any goals.

Sidelines Also known as a touchline, these are either of the two longer sides of the field rectangle.

Soccer Age Where a player's skill level and understanding of the game falls relative to other players. Younger siblings of other soccer players often have a greater soccer age than does the average child of his chronological age.

Soccer Sense Intuition for where to be and how to pass during a game in a variety of situations.

"Square" Phrase used by one player to indicate to a teammate with the ball that they are directly to the side and are available to receive a pass.

Square Pass A lateral pass made directly to a player's immediate left or right.

Starters The group of players who start out on the field at the beginning of a game.

Stoppage Any situation requiring that the game be stopped, say for an injury or a foul.

Stoppage Time Time added at the end of a period of play to account for any stoppages that may have happened during that period. Two to five minutes per half is typical.

Strip Another name for a player's full uniform, usually understood to consist of a color-coordinated jersey, shorts, and socks. See also Kit.

Studs See Cleat Studs.

Subs Abbreviation for substitutes.

Substitutes Players who are not currently on the field of play during the game.

Substitution The act of changing one player on the field for another.

Sudden Death See Golden Goal.

The Eighteen The edge of the penalty box closest to the center of the field. Applies, of course, only to regulation field sizes for which a penalty box measures 18 x 44 yards, but is sometimes used even on fields with different dimensions.

Through-Pass A pass to a teammate who is running into the space behind a defender.

Throw-In Used to restart play when the ball has gone out of bounds on either touchline. It is awarded to the opponents of the last team to touch the ball.

"Time" Phrase used to indicate to a player who either has possession of the ball or who is about to receive the ball that no defending player is in his immediate vicinity.

Top of the Box See The Eighteen.

Touch Degree of skill in ball handling.

Touchline See Sideline.

Tournament An organized event involving two or more games per team over a short period of time.

Trap Any of several methods used to bring the ball under control when receiving it over a distance. Common examples of traps include a chest trap or a thigh trap.

Yellow Card Visual signal from a referee indicating that a player has committed a "cautionable" offense. Depending upon specific leagues, a player may have to leave the field briefly when receiving the caution, but can return at the next substitution opportunity. Receiving a second yellow card in the same game will result in expulsion from the game.

11 Selected Resources for Further Reading

Allan, David. *Getting Things Done: The Art of Stress Free Productivity.* New York: Penguin, 2002.

American Academy of Pediatrics. "Guidelines for Pediatricians: Nutrition and Sports, Issue 6." https://www.aap.org/sections/sportsmedicine/PDFs/SportsShorts_06.pdf.

Arcelli, Enrico. *Nutrition for Soccer Players.* Spring City: Reedswain, 1997.

Bompa, Tudor. *Total Training for Young Champions: Proven Conditioning Programs for Athletes Ages 6 to 18.* Champaign: Human Kinetics, 2000.

Center for Disease Control and Prevention. "Heat Illness." http://www.nlm.nih.gov/medlineplus/heatillness.html.

Chastain, Brandi with Gloria Averbuch. *It's Not About the Bra: Play Hard, Play Fair and Put the Fun Back into Competitive Sports.* New York: HarperCollins, 2004.

Clark, Bobby. *The Baffled Parents Guide to Coaching Youth Soccer.* Camden: Ragged Mountain Press, 2000.

deLench, Brooke. *The Critical Role of Mothers in Team Sports.* New York: HarperCollins, 2006.

DiCicco, Tony and Colleen Hacker. *Catch them Being Good: Everything You Need to Know to Successfully Coach Girls.* New York: Penguin, 2002.

Edison, Emily. "Replenish, Rejuvenate, Recover, and Repeat," Play On!, Washington State Youth Soccer Association, April, 2009.

Federation Internationale de Football Association. "Laws of the Game." http://www.fifa.com/worldfootball/lawsofthegame.html.

Fish, Joel and Susan Magee. *101 Ways to be a Terrific Sports Parent.* New York: Fireside, 2003.

Hargreaves, Alan. *Skills and Strategies for Coaching Youth Soccer.* Champaign: Human Kinetics, 1990.

Lair, Cynthia. *Feeding the Young Athlete: Sports Nutrition Made Easy for Players and Parents.* Seattle: Moon Smile Press, 2002.

Lewis, Michael. *Soccer for Dummies.* Indianapolis: Wiley, 2000.

Luxbacher, Joe. *Soccer Practice Games.* Champaign: Human Kinetics, 2003.

National Institute of Arthritis and Musculoskeletal and Skin Diseases. "Sprains and Strains." http://www.niams.nih.gov/Health_Info/Sprains_Strains/default.asp.

Parker, Michael. *Premier Soccer: Skillls, Tactics and Strategies for Winning Play.* Champaign: Human Kinetics, 2008.

Pollack, William. *Real Boys: Rescuing Our Sons from the Myths of Boyhood.* New York: Henry Holt, 1998.

Schmid, Sigi and Bob Alejo. *Complete Conditioning for Soccer.* Champaign: Human Kinetics, 2002.

Smith, Dave, Pete Edwards and Adam Ward. *Step-by-Step Soccer Skills.* London: Hamlyn, 2000.

Ungerleider, Steven. *Mental Training for Peak Performance: Top Athletes Reveal the Mind Exercises They Use to Excel.* Emmaus: Rodale, 2005.

United States Soccer Federation. "2006 Youth Soccer Heat and Hydration Guidelines." http://www.ussoccer.com/common/stContent.jsp_51-MedInfo01.html.

United States Soccer Federation. "Best Practices for Coaching Soccer in the United States." http://images.ussoccer.com/Documents/cms/ussf/Best_Practices.pdf.

US Department of Health and Human Services. "Physical Activity Facts." http://www.fitness.gov/resources/facts/index.html.

Zimmerman, Jean and Gil Reavill. *Raising Our Athletic Daughters: How Sports Can Build Self-Esteem and Save Girls' Lives.* New York: Doubleday, 1998.

Useful Web Resources

In this section, you'll find a list of some of the many amazing resources available on the internet. Please recognize that as the internet is an ever-changing medium, some of these resources may have disappeared or be substantially changed by the time you read this. Don't let it stop you if anything is missing. Just type your question into your favorite search engine. Chances are you'll come up with a multitude of sites offering useful information. The information is out there, so there's no excuse to be in the dark! Curiosity is a good thing.

Soccer Resources

Federation Internationale de Football Association (FIFA), the Official Governing Body for Soccer in the World: http://www.fifa.com.

United States Soccer, the Official Governing Body for Soccer in the United States: http://www.ussoccer.com/

United States Youth Soccer: http:/www.usyouthsoccer.org

US Club Soccer: http://www.usclubsoccer.org

American Youth Soccer Organization (AYSO): http://soccer.org

Your state youth soccer association (e.g. for Washington, it is www.wsysa.org)

Coaching Resources

United States Soccer Federation, Best Practices for Coaching Soccer (http://images.ussoccer.com/Documents/cms/ussf/Best_Practices.pdf)

National Soccer Coaches Association of American, http://www.nscaa.com/

United States Soccer Federation, National Coaching School (licensing and certifications): http://ussoccer.com/coaches/schools/index.jsp.html

Equipment Retailers

EuroSport: Soccer.com

Soccersaves.com

WorldSoccerShop.com

Health and Nutrition

United States Department of Agriculture, Nutritional Information: http://mypyramid.gov

Medline Plus, National Institute of Health: http://medlineplus.gov/

American Academy of Pediatrics: http://aap.org/

Mayo Clinic: http://mayoclinic.org

Parenting Resources

MomsTeam.com, though not specific to soccer, this website is a treasure trove of information for general sports parenting: http://momsteam.com.

Passback, a non-profit foundation that provides used soccer gear to underprivledged children: http://www.passback.org/

Google Calendar, online shared calendar: http://www.google.com/intl/en/googlecalendar/about.html

eTeamz, team website hosting service: http://www.eteamz.com/

PlainWhitePress.com/4Moms